KT-525-433

My Lynda

Losing and loving my beloved wife,
Lynda Bellingham

MICHAEL PATTEMORE

**SIMON &
SCHUSTER**

London · New York · Sydney · Toronto · New Delhi

A CBS COMPANY

First published in Great Britain by Simon & Schuster UK Ltd, 2015
This paperback edition first published in Great Britain
by Simon & Schuster UK Ltd, 2016
A CBS COMPANY

1 3 5 7 9 10 8 6 4 2

Simon & Schuster UK Ltd
1st Floor
222 Gray's Inn Road
London WC1X 8HB

www.simonandschuster.co.uk

Simon & Schuster Australia, Sydney
Simon & Schuster India, New Delhi

The author and publishers have made all reasonable efforts to contact
copyright-holders for permission, and apologise for any omissions or errors
in the form of credits given. Corrections may be made to future printings.

A CIP catalogue record for this book
is available from the British Library.

Paperback ISBN: 978-1-4711-5176-7
Ebook ISBN: 978-1-4711-5177-4

Typeset in Garamond by M Rules
Printed and bound by CPI Group (UK) Ltd, Croydon, CR0 4YY

Simon & Schuster UK Ltd are committed to sourcing paper
that is made from wood grown in sustainable forests and support the Forest
Stewardship Council, the leading international forest certification organisation.
Our books displaying the FSC logo are printed on FSC certified paper.

They say it's better to have loved and
lost than never to have loved at all
and I have to agree, B.
I wish to God I hadn't had to lose you. But,
without a shadow of a doubt, you gave me
the best ten years of my life. I love you
today as much as I did yesterday. Until we
meet again, my lover, you will be in my
heart until the day I die.

x

ACKNOWLEDGEMENTS

......

First of all, I would like to say a huge thank you to all my family and Lynda's for the support they've given me on some very dark days this past year.

Jean, Michael, Stacey, Robbie, Brad and my stepbrother Michael, I appreciate and love you all, but I have to give a very special thank you to my son Brad for being there for me every single day. You still are and it means the world to me.

Writing this book has been important for me but, needless to say, it hasn't always been easy, and there are a number of people I want to thank who have helped me say what I wanted to say. It has meant so much to me that many of those people were close to Lynda, too, and friends of us both.

I could not have written this book without the support of Carole Richardson who, before any words were even put down on paper, knew so much about what Lynda and I thought about things and what we had lived through together and who, as a result, had such a wonderful instinct for getting everything together in the way I felt it should be said. I'm also so grateful to Gordon Wise, Lynda's literary agent at Curtis Brown. Gordon, as he did with Lynda, knew what it was that I wanted to achieve in telling this story, and worked closely with Sue Latimer, Lynda's talent agent at ARG, who looked after Lynda for so much of her acting career. Suzanne Baboneau at Simon & Schuster has been as supportive an editor for me as she was with Lynda on her novels. I value my personal relationships with these four just as much as I value our professional ones. Suzanne's team at Simon & Schuster, including Emma Harrow in Publicity and also a very patient design and production department, and Lynda's and my wonderful copyeditor Charlotte Cole, have genuinely made this book possible. I also want to take this moment to thank all of the amazing publishing professionals who have been part of taking Lynda's message out into the world.

Last, but by no means least, I would like to thank all the phenomenal staff at the cancer charities I am fortunate enough to have become involved with in the wake of this personal tragedy. Before Lynda's death, we were both supporters of her oncologist Professor Justin Stebbing's Action Against Cancer, which funds research to develop cures for this dreadful disease.

More recently, I have also become a patron of Bowel Cancer UK, which works hard to save lives by raising awareness, campaigning for the best treatment and care, and providing practical support and advice. Early diagnosis is vital and it is essential that the right information gets across to the public, so their work is crucial. Survival rates in the UK are amongst the lowest in Europe, with 15 per cent more patients diagnosed at a later stage of the disease compared to most other European countries. Every year, thousands, like Lynda, die unnecessarily. I salute the devoted individuals working tirelessly to put a stop to this and it is a privilege to support you in Lynda's memory.

CONTENTS

......

PART ONE

PART TWO

Part One

CHAPTER 1

THE MORNING AFTER

......

Still half asleep, my arm reaches across the bed and for that split second everything's okay. Then I come to and I suddenly remember. She's not here . . .

I get up straight away and the first thing I see is Lynda's open handbag under the big desktop computer in our bedroom, where she wrote her four books. Lying right at the top is the tan leather Filofax diary she lived by. And I lose it completely. I've no idea how long I sit there in her chair, stark naked, just staring at it and sobbing my heart out.

How many times had I tried to teach her to use an electronic diary to keep track of her appointments? She was always on the move my famous wife, the actress, author, charity campaigner and, for the past sixteen months, terminal cancer patient.

She had every conceivable piece of modern technology going: laptop, iPad, iPhone. I'd set it all up for her but it was a waste of time. It went in one ear and straight out the other.

'But, Michael, I love the quill,' she'd say, and every year I'd give in and buy her a new diary. Never again.

I knew, in my heart of hearts, I knew that Lynda wouldn't make it to Christmas, as she'd desperately hoped, but I honestly hadn't expected her to go when she did. Last night at 7.50 p.m., Sunday, 19 October 2014, not at home as we'd planned, but in my arms at the London Clinic. I thought she had another month, six weeks even, and might just make it into December and the start of the season she loved so much. But it wasn't to be.

Lynda's agent, Sue Latimer, has put out a statement letting the world know she'd died so, by nine o'clock this morning, reporters are on the doorstep of our first floor north London apartment wanting comments from me. The intercom phone is ringing off the hook. I must have answered and slammed it straight back down twenty times before I snap and tell the latest caller to foxtrotcharlie off.

A familiar voice is at the other end this time, though.

'It's me, Michael, your brother,' he says, and I press the buzzer to let my stepbrother up to where me and Lynda have lived for nearly six years with my son, Bradley, and Lynda's youngest son, Robbie. Her eldest boy, Michael, the actor, lives in a flat with his mates, and my daughter, Stacey, lives down in Warminster in the West Country with my young grandsons, Cooper and Oakley.

Upstairs, Brad and Robbie are still sleeping. None of us got to bed much before 4 a.m. The first thing I did when I arrived home from hospital, around midnight, was to head straight to the fridge to grab a bottle of Chablis, then another and another . . . We must have got through four or five bottles between the three of us, plus some vodka and whisky, as we sat round the dining table, talking and crying into the early hours, as I imagine every other devastated family does in our position. Mulling over life with Lynda, facing up to life without Lynda. How the hell would we cope?

My stepbrother, another Michael, walks into our open plan living room, hugs me, and I bawl my eyes out as I hug him back.

I don't think I was even dressed at that point. I don't even own a pair of pyjamas; I've never worn them since I joined the army's Junior Leaders at fifteen and I don't bother with a dressing gown. If I need to wander out of the bedroom before getting a shower in the en-suite bathroom, I've always just wrapped a towel round me in case I bump into the boys. I must have done the same that morning because I vaguely remember leaving Michael to keep guard on the door buzzer while I had a shower, shaved, put on a clean shirt and jeans, ready to face the day. My first as a widower. How I hate that word even now.

There was plenty to do, which would have pleased Lynda. She knew I'd need to keep busy if I was going to ever manage without her. Aside from cooking, which I hold my hand up to being completely useless at, it wasn't so much the practical stuff she was worried about. She knew I could clean up and run a tidy ship, but she knew the boys had their own lives and she didn't want me to be lonely when she'd gone. For ten wonderful years we'd always been inseparable. Up to now.

There is no fear of me being alone today, though, as people start to arrive to pass on their condolences and remember Lynda with us: close family and friends, including Michael and Robbie's old childhood nanny, Alena, and her two children.

In a daze, I run through in my mind what needs doing before I head off back to see Lynda in hospital and meet up with Clive, the funeral director, who is travelling up from Crewkerne, my old hometown in Somerset, to take her back with him.

Our family has known and trusted Clive for years and I didn't want anyone else laying her to rest in the beautiful hillside cemetery down there. I'd bought a double plot for us both four years ago when I was burying my father, Joe. That was long before 2 July 2013, the day that Lynda was diagnosed with bowel cancer.

As a practical man, I start to gather together the outfit she is to be buried in, the one she wore to receive her OBE at Buckingham Palace in March that same year. Within no time I've located the navy blue dress but, for the life of me, I can't find those bloody expensive shoes she loved so much. Unable to find a pair that matched the shade of her ivory coat perfectly, she'd had one handmade at massive expense, but now they are nowhere to be found.

The smaller fourth bedroom next to ours had been turned into a dressing room and I'd fitted a huge, open-fronted cupboard, where all our shoes were stored on separate Ikea metal rods. All except the ones I now want.

Suddenly, for the second time today, the habits of the past decade kick in. The same arm that automatically reached across the bed for her – as it has done every morning we'd woken up together – starts to move again.

Of its own accord, my left hand grabs my mobile and my thumb naturally hovers above number one to speed dial Lynda. What other number could she ever be?

Just in time, I stop myself from touching the screen to

call and ask her, 'Where the hell are your bloody shoes?' Sobbing, I sit back down on the dressing room sofa and start to wonder if this is how it's always going to be from now on. Will I ever come to accept that she's really gone; my Lynda, my B, my little Brontosaurus, my lover and my soulmate? And will I ever really want to?

CHAPTER 2

WHY ME?

......

I'm reminded of my own shortcomings every time I go to buy a new suit. At five foot eight inches, I always have to get the trousers and jacket sleeves altered because they're way too long. Little arms and legs; not a lot going for me!

So how the hell did I land Lynda in the first place, you might well ask? Why would a famous, beautiful actress like her (I'm not going to say celebrity because she hated that word), fall for a guy from Somerset like me? The honest truth is that I have absolutely no idea and it baffles me to this day.

As Bogart said in the film *Casablanca*: 'Of all the gin joints, in all the towns, in all the world, she walks into mine.'

I'm no Bogart but that's exactly how I felt when me and

Lynda first met outside a Spanish bar on 3 November 2004, in the tiny fishing town of Moraira on the Costa Blanca. I can remember it like it was yesterday and I gotta admit it: I fancied the pants off her. Straight away. No ifs or buts about it.

I'd moved to Spain early in 2001 after finding out that my first wife, Janice, had been having an affair. Walking straight out on almost twenty-five years of marriage, I'd arrived in Benidorm with jack shit. No money, no home, no job; just a suitcase in one hand and a credit card in the other.

I knew nothing at all about the property game, but I managed to get casual, commission-only work for a small company selling villas. I was a fast learner and soon picked up what an *escritura* was (title deeds are absolutely essential in Spanish property conveyancing) and moved on to a bigger organization with a head office about forty kilometres along the coast in beautiful Moraira.

Without meaning to sound snobby, it was more expensive, upmarket and cosmopolitan than Benidorm; not somewhere you could get a package holiday to, for instance. I fell in love with the place, which was conveniently slap bang between Alicante and Valencia airports, meaning there were always plenty of flights going back and forth to the UK. That was to come in very handy later when, for a good few years, I was commuting from north London.

I'm not boasting or bragging when I say I'm a natural entrepreneur, because it's true. It always has been, ever since I was wheeling and dealing in pushbikes as a kid. I like earning a few quid. Since I was twenty, I've been self-employed and I've loved every minute of it. So I figured out pretty quickly that business would be better up there in Spain. As soon as I'd learnt enough about the system, I found an office and set up my own company, The Mortgage and Property Shop.

Crucial to business was getting to know the local bar owners, who thankfully all spoke English – usually because they were Brits. Just as well, as I sure as hell couldn't speak much Spanish beyond the odd phrase like *hola* or *tres vino tintos* – hello and three red wines!

It was Richard, one of these bar owners, who'd phoned me the night before I met Lynda. I'd spent many a happy hour downing a few bottles of Riscal and Rioja with him and the locals over the past three years. I'd worked hard, though, and I'd earned a good name for my business.

'The Oxo bird is in town and her mate is looking for a mortgage,' he told me, tipping me off to a potential new bit of business.

*

Of course I knew instantly who he meant. Everybody remembers those iconic Oxo TV adverts of the 1980s and 90s, and Lynda as the mum they all wanted. But, much as I'd like to pretend differently here, they'd had absolutely no effect on me. They were always on in the background; I just never paid any attention. Sorry, B (I never liked calling her by her nickname Bellie so I either shortened it or lengthened it to 'my little brontosaurus').

I do now; often re-running them to catch my favourite bits. When we moved into our apartment, Lynda must have had a hundred or more video tapes of all the stuff she'd been in, from *All Creatures Great and Small* to *Doctor Who*, *The Bill* and *At Home with the Braithwaites*. I transferred them onto DVDs and they're all stored on shelves in the study.

'What kind of state are they in?' I asked Richard, wondering if I should go down to the bar and meet them that evening.

'They're knocking back double vodkas ...' he replied and I decided to wait until the next day to make my introductions.

'Tell them I'll see them at IG10 at 1.30 tomorrow afternoon. Tell them not to be late because the bank closes at two,' I said. Richard's bar didn't open at lunchtime and IG10 was another bar round the corner. It wouldn't give us much time, but I couldn't get there any earlier. Romance was the last thing on my mind in any case. I'd been seeing someone on and off for about a year, although it wasn't serious and we both had separate villas.

Five minutes after a phone call from Lynda's best friend, Pat Hay, the next afternoon – a Wednesday – I was pulling up outside a bar in my bright red BMW Z3 soft top. My 'hairdresser's car', as Lynda later christened it. She teased the life out of me for that motor.

Little did I know that she'd turned to Pat as I parked up and whispered, 'Oh my God, look at him. He's been round the block a few times. He looks like a right Jack the Lad!' (Honestly I'm not!)

'Yes, Bellie, and you'll probably have had him by Christmas!' Pat apparently replied, as they sat outside in the sunshine with another couple, tucking into a full English all-day breakfast. Lynda looked a little worse for wear, to say the least. She was dressed smartly in a white blouse and black trousers, if I remember rightly, but she had no make-up on so there was no disguising the fact that she had a hangover.

'I know who you are; I am Michael,' I said, pulling up

a chair and looking straight into Lynda's warm and kind but at the same time sexy brown eyes, and feeling an immediate attraction. Call me arrogant or vain, but I could sense, purely instinctively, that she felt it as well. Cleverer men with words than I am might have the right expression for what was happening between us. Thunderbolt? Spark? Electricity? Lust or love? It doesn't really matter. Whatever the feeling was, it was a two-way thing, intimate and so very real. Yet completely unexpected. Completely.

During my first marriage, I'd never ever strayed, not even once. Hand on heart. I could have done thousands of times when I was in the nightclub game, but I am quite proud of the fact I didn't. Just as I've never done drugs. After the marriage ended, it was another story (though not with the drugs. To this day, I've not even had one sniff of cocaine).

And I can honestly say that I never went looking for love again. There'd been a fair few women in and out of my bed since my divorce, particularly in lively old Benidorm which is teeming with fun-loving female holidaymakers. But, with apologies to the previous lady in my life, I can also tell you that Lynda was the first woman in a good few years who had really excited me. No question.

Business had to come first, though, and I turned to Pat. 'You must be the one looking for a mortgage.'

'Yes,' she replied. 'This is my sister Alma and her husband Robert.' She turned to the couple with them.

I asked her a few quick questions about her finances and, two minutes later, pointing to my car, said, 'Right, let's get going.' With the bank closing at 2 p.m., there was no time for pleasantries just yet.

Apparently, I discovered later, Pat's sister and brother-in-law expressed concern that I might have been whisking Pat off to join the slave trade, but Lynda must have instinctively trusted me now she'd met me as she told them she didn't think that was at all likely.

It didn't take long for Antonio, the bank manager, to arrange the small mortgage that Pat needed to buy the townhouse in Moraira she had her heart set on, and within no time we were back at the bar with the others.

'Would you like a drink?' Lynda offered. I didn't need asking twice. She ordered me a bottle of Budweiser and I sat down next to this sexy woman who I felt so immediately drawn to.

Now I am the first to admit that I am 100 per cent a red-blooded male, but it wasn't just that Lynda was so sexy and such an attractive lady. She had a lovely way with her as well. I'd sold villas to a few so-called 'celebrities' and, if you'll excuse the language, they were all a bit up their own arses. Since then, of course, I've met a lot more. Some of them I'd never want to meet again.

But Lynda was nothing like that. She was the real deal, giving off instant warmth and coming across as a genuine, lovely woman, the sort every man dreams of. Time would bear this out: here was nothing at all wrong with my first instincts.

Like a teenage boy in love for the first time, I drank my beer and accepted Lynda's offer of another one as I put on a professional front and raised the question of NIE numbers, which are similar to the National Insurance numbers we have in the UK.

There was no way that Pat or Lynda – who I learnt was buying a one-bed apartment by the sea but didn't need a mortgage – would be able to own a property without these numbers, and their estate agent should have advised them this was the case.

'We don't know what you're talking about, Michael,' Lynda replied.

Aware that the two of them were flying back to London first thing the following morning, I explained that they'd have to return to Spain to sort it out officially.

I'll never forget the look of horror on Lynda's face as she told me she was about to start rehearsals for the play, *Losing*

Louis, at Hampstead Theatre and she wouldn't be able to take any time off.

Then, of course, I didn't know anything about strict theatre contracts or how seriously Lynda took her profession. She loved being an actress and would never let anybody down. Work always came first with her.

Looking back now, I can see that was one of the many things we had in common: our strong work ethic. We both believed that either you do the job right or you don't do it at all. I've never in my life been afraid of grafting and nor was Lynda. Nothing came on a plate to either of us. I started off my working life in the building trade as a roofer, which anybody in the property game will tell you is real hard graft. In the early days, between acting parts, Lynda worked as a cleaner to pay her rent and eat, even if it meant that sometimes she could only stretch to boiled eggs and toast.

The only difference between us was that, whatever I've done – from building houses to owning nightclubs – I have always worked first and foremost to make money. I'm not ashamed to admit I like having money and what it can buy. But if I lost it all tomorrow it wouldn't bother me because I'd just start all over again. I've made a million, lost a million and made it again. I'm a survivor.

With Lynda, whenever acting was concerned, it was all about her craft. The job, the role, came first, the fee second. I must admit it took me a while to get my head round that, although I like to think that I did make her a bit more savvy about the business side of showbiz. Not that I ever interfered with what she did or, for the record, ever lived off her money. Ever. I've never needed to. She did her thing; I did mine.

I waited that afternoon in Moraira while Lynda made a few phone calls – one to the play's director as far as I can recall – and then announced, to everybody's relief, that they could actually fly back the following Monday.

I arranged to meet them at 8.30 a.m. that day outside Pat's sister's place, which was just around the corner from Richard's bar.

'Please don't be late,' Lynda pleaded. As if! I was already hooked and I knew I wouldn't be able to wait for Monday. Five whole days away. That was another thing I didn't know about her at the time: she was a stickler for timing. She hated being late herself and didn't appreciate other people keeping her waiting. In her book, it was just bad mannered, if not downright rude.

Her former colleagues on *Loose Women* will tell you that Lynda was always the first to arrive at briefing meetings with the producer before the show, notes in hand. On occasion she'd been known to knock on dressing room doors and, in no uncertain terms, tell some of the others on the panel to get a move on.

Not a problem, I promised her, and, not wanting to outstay my welcome, I felt it was time to leave. Thanking them for the beers, I drove off reluctantly, looking forward to our next meeting and feeling as excited as if we'd just arranged a romantic dinner date, rather than a trip to the local police station to get boring but very necessary NIE numbers. Later on I was to learn that Lynda herself was already pretty smitten too.

Monday morning arrived and it was a really beautiful day. I pulled up at Alma's apartment bang on time, though not on this occasion in my hairdresser's car as I'd swapped vehicles for the day with the lady in my life at the time.

'At least you're not late,' Lynda said, climbing into the back of my borrowed grey Citroën Picasso.

Same to you, darling, I thought to myself, even if I didn't actually say it.

Pat sat beside me in the front and Lynda in the back, where, there was no doubt about it, she was sussing me out. I could see her looking at me in the rear-view mirror. Every time I glanced at it, she was looking straight back at me as she chatted away nineteen to the dozen.

'Do you have a lady in your life?' she asked.

'Sort of,' I replied and she came straight back at me.

'What do you mean "sort of"?'

I explained as briefly as I could that, yes, there was a lady but it wasn't going anywhere.

'Why's that?' she demanded to know and, desperate to change the subject, I told her I wasn't in love before asking, as casually as I could, 'No husband?'

'That's a long story, Michael, but not a car ride story. I'll tell you another time,' she promised.

Intrigued or maybe even a bit desperate for there not to be, I asked, 'Well, is there a man in your life?'

'No,' was her answer and the one I most definitely wanted to hear. *Hmm, you never know Michael*, I smiled to myself as I carried on driving to the city police station at Dénia, a thirty-minute drive away, continuing to look in my rear-view mirror a bit more often than was strictly necessary.

The conversation in the car was light and easy, completely spontaneous. That was something else that me and Lynda had in common. We liked to jump in with both feet and get things done, often on a whim. Lynda was by far the worst. If she wanted a new car and walked into a showroom to find they had the right model but not in the right colour, she wouldn't wait for it to be ordered. Where I'd always wait, patient to get what I wanted, Lynda would take the different coloured one because, once she'd made up her mind, she had to have it there and then.

There was many a time, I admit, when I'd wished she hadn't been quite so spontaneous. Usually it was in John Lewis and around Christmas time! Just how many Christmas decorations does a home need? More than we could ever possibly use or even store, it seemed. God, what I'd give right now to wake up in the morning, discover it had all been a bad dream, and find her lying beside me again. I'd happily carry her all the way to Oxford Street and she could buy the whole bloody store up if she wanted to. Anything to have her back. Even for one day.

The light flirting in the car continued and I found myself asking Lynda how old she was, but she'd only reply, 'A lot older than you.'

'I don't think so, Babes,' I said.

'I know so!' she laughed.

'Tell me,' I asked again.

'I'm not telling you . . .' and on it went with me, teasing her that I'd find out anyway in the next half hour when she had to hand over her passport at the police station. Once we arrived, I grabbed it off her and after doing a quick bit of mental arithmetic managed to work out that she was fifty-six, not that she looked it despite having had no cosmetic work done since she had a nose job early on in her career.

I was forty-nine at the time, with all my own teeth and a full head of hair. Thanks to a good dentist I've still got my own teeth, but my hair has needed a bit of help over the last three years and, a few months ago, I travelled to Dublin for a transplant, just as me and Lynda had planned. If she really is up there looking down on me, I wonder what she thinks? I believe, without a shadow of a doubt, that she is up there watching.

Lynda was a great believer in the afterlife and I always knew that if she had any way of communicating with me, she would do so. I like to believe she has. She used to joke to one of the journalists at *Yours* magazine, where she had a popular fortnightly column for six years, right up to her death, that when she was no longer around she'd send her messages down from above to readers. 'Or they may be coming upwards,' she once laughed last summer after she'd made the decision, when things got really tough, to stop her chemo. 'One can't assume!'

Sorry, Babes, but you got it wrong there. There's only one place you were ever going when you left us and it wasn't anywhere red hot and full of smoke!

It's fair to say that we both took a pride in our appearance. Obviously, it was important that Lynda always looked her best because of her public image. You never knew round which corner a photographer might be lurking. Being Lynda, she took it in her stride and was usually pleasant even if she didn't always entirely appreciate the intrusion, especially towards the end. But she was canny as well, and knew that the day she was no longer newsworthy was probably the day she would no longer be working in the business. And that was unthinkable to her.

As for me, I've always liked to look smart. I wear jeans 90 per cent of the time but they're always clean, usually Levis, tailored to fit me properly. I also have a real penchant for nice designer shirts and jackets, and I only buy shoes with leather soles that I keep shiny and polished. I always used to polish Lynda's shoes for her as well. It's a bit of a habit with me that probably goes back to the two years that I spent in the army when I was a teenager.

Lynda used to say that I liked only the best and she was bang on there. With her I got the very best ten years of my life. We had an absolute ball together. Just phenomenal. But of course that makes it much harder now, finding myself so alone without her.

Some days, but never Sundays, are better than others of course. However, they all have one thing in common: not a single day goes by when I don't cry. Even now, I could sit at home all day and cry for her – but what good's that going to do? So I try to plan ahead and get out as much as possible. But then someone might recognize me as Lynda's husband, in the street or the supermarket, and tell me how sorry they are for my loss. Those are probably the worst moments, with people I don't even know. Everybody has been so kind, more than kind. And that's when I really lose it and the tears come.

Or it could be listening to Lynda's famous sexy actress's voice. I've had it on my voicemail for years, telling callers in that very naughty, exaggerated and suggestive tone of hers: 'I'm so sorry but we're frightfully busy at the moment and can't come to the phone right now.'

After she died, it used to bring her right back and keep her alive in such a real way. I was so desperate not to lose the message that I tried to copy it onto my Dictaphone for posterity. While I was messing about I managed to wipe it out altogether. I was gutted. I've managed to find another message that she did as a voicemail message for our home phone and I've transferred that, but it's not as much fun. Still, I suppose I'm luckier than most because I have so much to choose from. If I want to hear her voice again, I only have to pick up a DVD.

I really can't imagine that I would ever want to hear another woman's voice on my answerphone, whatever the future holds and whoever I might find myself with. Lynda was adamant that I should find another woman after she left me, but we shall see. For months all I've been able to think is, *Why did it all have to end so soon, B?* We had such plans for the future. All buggered up by cancer. The Big Bloody C. But I can't let myself to get too bitter because Lynda was never bitter and, let's face it, she had the most cause. It was her life that was cut off in her prime with so much for her to look forward to, both with work and her family life.

So back to the happier start to the story ... If Lynda was here now, I know she'd be butting in and correcting me over every last detail, insisting that her version of events was right, not mine. But she's not here, and this is how I remember it, still so vividly, in my own mind.

The Spanish paperwork took about an hour to complete so the three of us left the police station and headed for a nearby bar until the NIE numbers were ready for us to collect.

Trust me, I never drink and drive today. I don't believe in it. At all. But in Spain, life was different and we ordered a glass of red wine. Then it suddenly dawned on me that Lynda would need to return to Spain to exchange contracts on the apartment she was buying. After what she'd said about the demands of the play, I sensed that it could be another problem for her. I suppose, though, what I really mean is that I realized that it would be another excuse to see her.

Not wanting to panic her, I asked, 'Tell me about the play.' Lynda explained that it was showing in Hampstead but she was hoping it would transfer to the West End after that run.

'How are you going to come back and buy your apartment?' I asked, explaining that the Spanish system wasn't like the one in England when you exchange contracts and complete without necessarily being present. She would need to see a notary, someone with legal training who is licensed by the government to carry out certain legal acts like witnessing a signature, in person, before reaching that stage.

'I can't do that. There's no way on earth I can come back so soon.' She sounded panic-stricken.

'You'd better give Pat power of attorney then,' I suggested, disappointed, and nodded in her friend's direction. Lynda agreed immediately.

'Plus we need to get you a bank account as well,' I added.

I had got to know Sue in the local notary office, so I gave her a quick call and asked for an appointment that afternoon to sort out the power of attorney.

'Michael, we're chock-a-block today. It ain't happening ...'

'Come on, Sue,' I begged.

'What's the name?' she sighed, sensing my desperation, and I told her.

'Not the Oxo one?' she enquired.

'Yeah.'

'She seems a lovely lady . . .'

'She is,' I assured her. And I meant it. Smitten already.

In all the years we were together, I can only recall one occasion when Lynda used her famous name to call in special favours and that was in an airport when she was touring with *Calendar Girls*. She was exhausted and the flight was delayed so she asked to go in the VIP lounge. Playing the 'Do you know who I am?' card just wasn't her style.

All the while we were sorting out Lynda's bank account and power of attorney, we were laughing and giggling like two love-struck kids. Non-stop banter and flirting. Plus a fair few dirty jokes. She was so funny. Pat joined in with the joking. If she felt awkward in any way, she didn't show it.

As TV sitcom writer and friend, Jan Etherington, said of Lynda at her memorial: 'She was a natural clown as well, which is so rare in a beautiful woman. She could fall over the back of a sofa with as much grace as she could dance on *Strictly*.'

In short, you were a one-off, B, even if you never quite had the self-confidence – though God only knows why – to see it for yourself. Psychologists could have had a field day with the pair of us, I'm sure. Relationship counsellors would have struggled if they'd had to rely on couples like us for business, though. We had such a fantastic relationship both in and out of the bedroom. I honestly cannot recall a single argument between us in ten whole years.

Lynda wanted to see where I was living and I drove her out to my villa, dropping off poor Pat, who didn't seem to mind too much, in a local bar on the way.

When we arrived, I realized that I hadn't got my house keys with me as, of course, I'd swapped cars for the day with the woman I was sort of seeing and they were on the same keyring.

Lynda looked at me in such a way and I just knew it for certain. I knew I wasn't imagining any of the feelings between us. It was so normal and so instant. No ifs or buts, we'd just clicked. It's hard to explain but it was like meeting your first ever love and soulmate.

Had I had those keys to that villa, I am certain we'd have ended up in bed together that day. In fact I know it.

I'd told Lynda the truth that morning when I'd said the relationship I was in wasn't going anywhere. Don't get me wrong, she was a nice lady. The relationship had become something of a habit. I did what I wanted to do most of the time and so did she.

One of the things I am proud of about myself is that I don't tell lies and never have. I get that from my dad, who was as honest as the day was long. Had it been a different story and I'd been serious about my lady friend, I'd have admitted it there and then. Lynda would not have crossed the line either. We would not have gone any further. She had strong moral views on that sort of thing, as did I. Remember I'd had my own fingers burnt not that long beforehand ...

Finding myself alone with Lynda again that afternoon, we talked about the fun things in life; nothing too serious like her previous marriage, or mine for that matter. All the heavy, personal stuff was yet to come.

I'll never forget walking from one bar to the other when she put her arm in mine and asked, 'So, if I come over here quite regularly, will you look after me?'

'Just a bit, Babes!' I replied chirpily, grinning from ear to ear.

Just as well, though, that I'd mentioned the lady in my life at that time. Earlier the two of us had arranged to meet up in the same bar I found myself in with Lynda. Both looked a bit shocked to see the other.

Afterwards I learnt that Lynda had been expecting a six foot, busty blonde, but she was nothing like that. Glam in her own way, she always dressed well and turned men's head, but was well under five feet tall (okay, maybe I'm exaggerating a bit) and very fit, and athletic looking. She had no meat on her whatsoever.

Feeling more than a little embarrassed sitting there with Lynda and Pat, who'd rejoined us by then, I bought everybody a drink and made a few awkward introductions before realizing it was time to leave with my lady friend.

I thought Lynda was just being polite when she said to me, 'Whenever you're in London, give me a shout and I'll take you out for a meal.'

We kissed each other – just friendly pecks on either side of the cheek – and I left. It's true to say that when I walked out of that bar and drove off, I didn't think I'd ever see Lynda again. I thought that was it. Let's face it, we were both from completely different worlds. Completely and utterly.

Of course, back then I didn't realize just how much we had in common either. Lynda was brought up mainly in rural Aston Abbotts in Buckinghamshire, by her retired pilot father, Don, and mum, Ruth. She had two younger sisters, Barbara and Jean, and her idyllic middle-class life on the farm came complete with her precious pony Tiddlywinks.

I was born in Musgrove Park Hospital in Taunton, Somerset, on 18 August 1955. If you do the maths you'll realize that, by the time you're reading this, I'll have turned sixty without Lynda here to produce my customary chocolate birthday cake – the only dessert I really like. We had such plans to celebrate my birthday together. Lynda would have finished the Kay Mellor play, *A Passionate Woman*, in which she was starring with another of her old screen-husband Christopher Timothy. He was the vet James Herriot when she was Helen, in *All Creatures Great and Small*, long before in 1978.

She'd been offered the part in *A Passionate Woman* shortly before she was diagnosed and was devastated that she couldn't go ahead with it, bless her heart. After the initial year-long regional tour, we were hoping to take a month or six-week long holiday going round most of the world together. Up to that point we'd both been too busy with work commitments to do much travelling for fun. But of course it wasn't to be.

Unlike Lynda's, my own childhood wasn't quite so picture book.

I was only a few months old when my real mum walked out after she and my dad fell out. I was their only child and he tried to bring me up himself at first. But he couldn't cope with working as a mechanic to pay the bills and looking after a baby at the same time. Reluctantly, he had to have me fostered when I was a year old.

What I didn't know when I met Lynda – and the rest of the world didn't know either – was that she'd been rejected by her own birth mother as well. Born Meredith Lee Hughes in Montreal, Canada, on 31 May 1948, Lynda was adopted six months later and brought back to England by Ruth and Don. Unfortunately I never met either of her adoptive parents, which was a real shame and I know that it was something Lynda deeply regretted.

I'm no expert, but maybe that goes some way to explaining that basic deep connection between us as well as some of the character traits we shared.

For a start, and although it might sound daft to say it now, Lynda, like me, was a born survivor. Beaten only by cancer, though of course you could argue that that fucking disease never managed to break her spirit.

We both had addictive personalities and were completely driven. Me by money; Lynda by acting success, but success and fame were completely different things in her book. She had no time at all for people who wanted to be famous for the sake of being famous.

When we weren't working, it was play, play, play, just as much as it was work, work, work when we were busy. We thrived on it. It was good for both of us; it worked well. Phenomenal. Just phenomenal.

We were also very positive people as well, although

Lynda was more of a worrier. 'You are my Mr Positive,' she used to say to me. Even when my spirit was tested big time by her cancer, I really thought that together we'd beat it. For a long time.

And, like Lynda, the whole celebrity thing doesn't impress me two hoots, so my head was never turned in the first place by the fact that she was an actress. In truth, when we met she was in a bit of a desert workwise. Her star was yet to rise again when she landed *Loose Women* and *Calendar Girls*. From the word go, I just loved being in her company.

I didn't wear my heart on my sleeve quite as much as Lynda, though, and sometimes, I've got to admit, she did drive me mad with her openness; telling everything to everybody. Now it wouldn't bother me. To be fair, I admit that I am an open book myself, always have been. I might have a head for business and making money but I am also very emotional, especially where family and friends are concerned.

Looking back, it was nothing short of a miracle that me and Lynda – and our two families – hit it off like we did. Stacey and Brad, Michael and Robbie are all very different characters with different experiences of life, but they came together and we all got on so well, which isn't always the case with stepfamilies.

*

But first, long before we reached that stage, there was something very important that I needed to get off my chest that could make or break this blossoming new relationship in one fell swoop. As I said earlier, I am an honest man so it had to be brought out into the open. And I was not looking forward to it. Not one little bit . . .

CHAPTER 3

EMPTY ROOMS

......

Walking back into our silent north London apartment, the first thing I see is a bunch of white lilies in a tall glass vase on the dining room table. Across the far side of the open-plan kitchen and living area I clock another one, almost identical, on the coffee table.

For the first time in my life, at fifty-nine, I am a man who's buying flowers for himself, not for a wife, a girlfriend or a mother. Every fortnight, I've started to go into our local supermarket and spend the best part of twenty quid on a couple of fresh bunches. I bring them home, chuck out the old ones and rinse the vases before putting the flowers in water and placing them in vases in the exact same spots. If they're looking a bit worse for wear before two weeks is up, I do it sooner.

It became a bit of a ritual that started shortly after I threw away all the sympathy flowers we'd been sent. There must have been at least twenty vases and it was no five-minute job. But at least it kept me occupied on a gloomy Sunday morning in early November, the day before Lynda's funeral, when all I could think about was burying my beloved wife and whether everything would go to plan. I wanted it all to be perfect.

Bouquets were always arriving for Lynda throughout our time together, but never more so than during the last few weeks when the news broke that her cancer was terminal – just three weeks to the day before I lost her. She loved fresh flowers, and when they weren't being given to her she'd buy her own and the place was never without them. She usually bought lilies but, whatever kind of bloom they might be, they were always white and green. She had quite strict rules about that if she or the family was buying them for home. Not as strict as the one she had about garage forecourt flowers, though. Woe betide the boys if they bought her a scraggy last-minute bunch for Mother's Day or her birthday.

As she always said, she'd rather have nothing than a gesture that was so obviously an afterthought. A visit and maybe a card – in that order – was all she really wanted. Having her family celebrating round the dinner table – usually eating a meal she'd cooked herself – meant everything to her.

I never intended the flowers I suddenly found myself buying to become a shrine to Lynda. Even now, I have a monthly standing order with Bee Floral in Yeovil, who supplied the lovely sprays and wreaths for her funeral. Clive the funeral director had recommended them and they haven't disappointed me yet. Every fortnight they put a fresh bunch of Lynda's favourite white lilies or sometimes white roses on her grave, which is protected from the wild rabbits down there by netting. They can be real greedy little buggers.

It was more that I had got used to having flowers in the apartment when Lynda was here, and I suppose they were my strange way of trying to keep things the same as before. Not that I ever could. But when you've just lost someone you loved so much, you're not really thinking straight and definitely not the same way you thought before.

Everybody who has been through a bereavement says that it is after the funeral that the full blown grief kicks in. Beforehand, there's too much to do and too many people around you. Afterwards they're gone and you're all on your own. It's suddenly quiet, empty and lonely at home. And it's a fact. The boys have been good, but they all have their own lives to lead. Not a problem. That's what me and Lynda both wanted.

I'd expected and, as much as you ever can be, I was sort of prepared for the quiet emptiness of the rooms without her there, laughing loudly, always full of sparkle and so much larger than life. Or so I thought.

Everywhere I look now reminds me of what I've lost, and nothing feels right or the same. Even Tiddlywinks, the wooden rocking horse I surprised her with for Christmas 2012, looks as sad and lonely as I'm now feeling, standing in the corner by the living room window.

I'll never forget how absolutely thrilled Lynda was when I gave her a tiny gift-wrapped box on Christmas morning. We were staying in a hotel in Bradford because she was appearing as the Fairy Godmother in the panto *Cinderella* with Billy Pearce, and she didn't have enough time off between performances to warrant travelling all the way home for only a few hours. Inside the box was a miniature rocking horse.

'Oh, Michael, isn't that beautiful! Big kiss!' she gushed, recognizing the intricate model from her *My Tasty Travels* series for ITV the previous summer. Lynda had travelled round in an old VW campervan, interviewing skilled crafts-men and women, as I tagged along behind. One of them was the man at Cockington Rocking Horses in Torquay, and I'd had a quiet word with him when she wasn't around . . .

I laughed at her shocked face when I told her that this wasn't her real Christmas present; a full-sized version was on order and would be arriving at home the following spring.

She'd loved the beautiful rocking horses when she watched them being made, each one by hand, and said how much she'd like one for the grandchildren. Up to then there was Michael's son, Sacha, and Stacey's boys, Cooper and Oakley. Of course Lynda hoped that one day she might see more arrive to ride Tiddlywinks. Not to be I'm afraid, my lover (this was Lynda's nickname for me, always spoken in a mimic West Country accent like mine).

All those hopes when, even then, without either of us knowing it, the cancer was already at work. It was the same Christmas that we'd ended up in casualty in Bradford after the second panto show on Christmas Eve. Lynda had been suffering from really bad indigestion and diarrhoea and was short of breath. When we finally saw a doctor, he said it was probably nothing and prescribed Omeprazole, a drug that reduces stomach acid, for a couple of weeks. She did so and it seemed to clear up. If only we'd known. As we found out later, though, it would probably have been too late even then.

I was really surprised to discover, after the funeral, that it was the actual smell of Lynda that I missed so much, especially on Sundays. Bloody Sundays.

Whether it's because Sundays used to be so great when we were together, or whether it's because I lost her on a Sunday and the bad memories take over, I can't say. All I know is that what was always the best day of our week immediately became my worst day. Overnight I started to hate Sundays; absolutely hate them.

The worst ever was the first Sunday after her funeral on 9 November 2014. I missed Lynda like crazy from the minute I woke up, still on the same side of our king-sized bed, the one nearest to the bedroom door in case burglars ever broke in. When I promised to always protect her in front of all her friends and family (a fair few of whom were dubious of me) in my wedding speech, I meant it literally.

To be fair, every morning since I lost her has started badly; still does. But weekdays and even Saturdays are busy generally. Places to go; people to see. Sundays spent at home alone stretch endlessly in front of me. Even if I've arranged to go out and meet somebody for lunch, Pat for instance, it's when I'm at my lowest.

Automatically, first thing in the morning, my arm still reaches across to the unrumpled, colder, empty side and then it's the smell of her I notice that is missing. Even first thing in the morning, Lynda always managed to smell gorgeous; I think it was the cream she used.

Unlike me, she didn't like showers; she loved a nice deep, old fashioned bath. I even took out the fancy spa one that was in here when we bought this place to install a normal bathtub. Every night at about 10 p.m. she'd lie in it for three quarters of an hour or so while I watched TV next door in the bedroom.

Once we had a laugh when the dress designer Vivienne Westwood admitted to the papers that she doesn't shower either and only baths in her husband's water. Lynda loved reminding me that when the country was hit by a serious drought in the summer of 1976, people were actually being advised to 'Save Water, Bath With A Friend' yet the only time she had offered me the tub after her, I'd turned my nose up.

'I'd have had no qualms getting in after you,' she half scolded. Neither would I now, Babes . . .

Sometimes I would go sit in the bathroom and chat to her as she relaxed in her bubbles or oils with scented candles all around her. She loved turning the lights off and lighting candles in the bathroom. It was actually very sexy when I look back.

Afterwards she'd smother herself in body cream. Don't ask me what brand it was. We both always bought our own toiletries. For me it was always Michael Kors, but Lynda had a lot of friends who sent her different gifts. The ones who knew her well knew she always emptied the last drop out of the bottle or tube. Though she could be extravagant and was ridiculously generous to everybody around her, she was never a waster with anything.

When I got up, that first Sunday morning after the

funeral, I headed out, as quickly as I could, to do my usual five-mile walk to check on one of my property developments. Maybe there was a problem with the plumbing that I needed to organize help with. Or, if the grass needed cutting, I'd mow the lawn – even though I hate gardening. Gardening wasn't something either of us was into. That's why we chose to live in an apartment on a complex where all that was taken care of for us.

Coming back into the apartment, I must have been in some sort of a daze because as soon as I walked through the door it hit me like a ton a bricks. There was no smell. Nothing. No crusty topped rack of lamb roasting to perfection. To die for, I always used to tell her. But not really of course. Funny how even silly everyday expressions that people have used harmlessly for years can pull you up short.

It's weird the way your senses completely take over your logical brain at times like this. Why on earth did I ever expect to arrive home to the delicious waft of Sunday lunch cooking when I'd buried my wife only six days earlier? Everything had changed now. Forever. *Get it into your thick head, Michael. Stop crying; pull yourself together.* After a solid hour and a half of pure wailing, I had to force myself to dry my eyes because I had an appointment with a new tenant in one of my rental properties. Otherwise, I think I'd have just sat there and sobbed all day and all night.

*

In the good old Sundays, of course, I'd be greeted by Lynda shouting, 'Hi my lover, your juice is made,' as she handed me a glass with all sorts of good stuff in it – celery, avocado, spinach and lemon juice. Full of vitamins. We got into the juicing habit a few years ago on a spa retreat in Majorca. It started off as a diet thing. Lynda never forgave me for losing ten pounds when she only lost nine herself! But because we seemed to have more energy when we drank it, we carried on. I still do it now. Well, most of the time.

As I drank the juice, we'd chat as she chopped and stirred, breaking off every few minutes to glance at the fancy cookbook she always had open on the worktop. Usually it was to check on the recipe for a dessert she was experimenting with. Or tasty stuff for the boys to eat in the week. She still liked to mother them all. Week in, week out she made a big jug of her speciality Italian tomato sauce like she'd been doing since Michael and Robbie were little boys. No matter how bad things got, she made that sauce all through her illness, right up to a couple of weeks before she died.

You've seen her in those Oxo advertisements; well that was the real Lynda. She was playing herself really. She could even make the best gravy, though I've got to be honest and say she that didn't always use Oxo cubes. A tipple of sherry in the pan was her secret weapon.

I've always said that whenever she walked through the

front door and closed it behind her, she was exactly the same person at home as the one people saw on the outside.

Everyone associated her with the Oxo mum – even if she didn't always appreciate it. She preferred to be remembered for her other, more serious, acting roles like Empress Alexandra Fyodorovna in the film *The Romanovs: An Imperial Family*. It was before my time but she'd told me all about going to Russia for the filming. Sadly, she never got to Hollywood and win the Oscar she'd dreamt of, but she never gave up hope. She had the talent for certain.

But Lynda wasn't daft. Far from it. She knew that, when she most needed the money, those sixteen years that the Oxo adverts ran paid the bills and the school fees for her boys.

In real life, she loved nothing more than getting the family and various friends – usually Pat, the boys and her sister Jean, and often her old chum Christopher Biggins – round the dining table and serving up a feast she'd cooked from scratch. Always from scratch. Self-taught, Lynda loved to experiment with food and, boy, could she cook!

Throughout the meal – and very unlike the TV Oxo mum – she'd entertain everyone with her jokes. Lynda could tell a joke like nobody else I know and, believe me, they could be filthy dirty! She had a wicked sense of humour and would have everybody in stitches as she delivered the punchlines with as much professionalism as if she'd been on stage. That was Lynda all over. Always aiming to give the best performance she could, whoever her audience was or how small it might be.

I have cooked myself the odd chicken breast or fillet steak with salad but I usually eat out on Sundays now. If truth really be told, I ate out most evenings for months, with my boy Brad when he was around – sushi more often than not. It's hard to stomach cooking for one, as often Brad and Robbie are out doing their own thing. That's what I want for them, but it does mean I'm home alone for hours on end, killing time like Billy No Mates.

It's funny how other habits changed as well. I can't really explain why, but I never seem to watch TV any more, which would help pass time. Before Lynda died, I'd always been a big TV watcher.

We used to watch it together every night. All the old stuff (we went through of real phase of re-running *Dallas*!), all the soaps: *Emmerdale, Coronation Street, EastEnders*, and all the American stuff on Netflix: *Breaking Bad, The Sopranos, House of Cards* and *Mad Men*.

If she was reading – Lynda was a real avid reader and would get through two or three books every week – I'd still watch it alone. It doesn't even cross my mind to do that now.

Thinking about it, it was books that kind of led us on to that second date – if you can call it that.

It must have been near the end of November 2004, and two or three weeks since I'd left Lynda and Pat in the bar. Lynda was back in the UK and I was in my villa in Spain. I'd just had a big argument with the lady I was seeing and walked out of her villa into the rain. It was bucketing down and I had a long walk back to Moraira from Javea.

Soaking wet, I ran a hot shower for myself the minute I got back to the villa. By 11 p.m. I was lying in bed with a Michael Connolly thriller. I liked his books. I don't know what made me do it but I picked up my phone and, on a whim, I found myself texting Lynda and asking, 'Hiya, Babes, how are you doing?'

Within seconds she replied, asking me what I was doing, so I told her that I was in bed reading a book.

'What are you reading?' she wanted to know. I texted back and she replied immediately: 'OMG that's one of my favourite authors. How many of his books have you read?'

On went the conversation thread as she explained she was in a Watford car park, supposedly making love to a guy during the filming of an episode of *Murder in Suburbia*! That was about as risqué as the texts got on that occasion if anybody had cared to read them. What was going on in both our minds was another story.

After patching things up a bit with my lady, we decided to fly back to England a few days before Christmas because she wanted to spend it in Manchester with her family. At that time, my ex-wife and Bradley were living in America. Stacey, who'd have been twenty-two by then, had had an argument with her husband-to-be Sam and I felt sorry for her being stuck on her own in Windsor for Christmas. I tried to book her a train ticket online but there was some problem so I decided to drive down from Manchester to get her.

I remember it as if it was yesterday: 23 December 2004. The weather was horrendous and the roads were a complete nightmare. Chock-a-block with traffic. I set off at 10 a.m. and didn't arrive in Windsor until 4 p.m.

A strange thing happened halfway down the motor-way – Lynda phoned me, expecting me to be in Spain. Completely out of the blue. She was enjoying a couple of glasses of wine with Pat when she decided to call and wish me a Happy Christmas. I swear she must have had a sixth sense.

We flirted shamelessly and she asked, 'Where are you? In Spain?'

'Believe it or not, I'm on the M6.'

The line went quiet before she asked if I was going anywhere near Highgate in north London, where she was living in a maisonette at the time with Michael and Robbie. They were away, though. Michael was in Italy with his father, Lynda's Italian ex-husband, Nunzio Peluso, and Robbie was in America with a friend and his family.

'I could do,' I replied, though I said it would depend on time because I had to get back to Manchester. I explained that I was going to book hotel rooms for me and Stacey for the night and we were going to head north the next morning.

Offering us dinner and a bed at her place Lynda said, 'Bring her with you.' Typical Lynda, generous to a fault, but in this case a little bit naughty too. She just wanted to get me over there and if that was what it took . . .

I carried on to collect Stacey, explained that we were staying with a 'friend' and we headed over to Lynda's. With no satnav, I didn't have a clue where we were going and had to rely on her directing us over the phone along the North Circular.

Eventually, more by luck than management, we pulled up outside her home in Avenue Road and she came out to meet us, looking amazing in tight jeans and a sweater. No ifs or buts, she was one gorgeous woman.

'Oh my god, I know who she is!' Stacey exclaimed. She'd recognized Lynda from watching *The Bill*.

Thrusting a glass of red wine into both our hands, Lynda announced, 'You've got to forgive me but it is the penultimate episode of *The Bill* on TV. I'm in it and I want to watch it.'

To the day I die I'll never forget looking at Lynda sitting in her own lounge and then at her character on the screen. In this case, she wasn't playing herself; she was playing the widowed villain, Irene Radford. Very different to the Oxo mum. It was bizarre. Absolutely surreal.

Afterwards we went into the kitchen where Lynda cooked us a delicious simple dinner of steak and chips as she plied my daughter with wine. I had a bloody good idea what she was up to. She wanted Stacey out of the way so that we could pick up where we'd left off in Spain.

It worked and, much worse for wear, Stacey went to bed in one of the boys' rooms while Lynda joined me in the lounge with another bottle of wine.

After we'd finished, she leaned over and kissed me.

Leading me down to her bedroom (where I admit I'd left my overnight bag just in case), we spent a phenomenal night together. Absolutely phenomenal. Pat had been right when she commented on that first meeting in Spain that Lynda would probably have 'had' me by Christmas. She had. Just!

Next morning, Lynda was in the bath and I was having a shave in the same bathroom. It was so normal; the two of us like an old married couple going through a normal morning's routine. It felt so right. Contented.

I didn't want to leave her and she didn't want me to go.

Had it not been for the fact that my passport was in Manchester, I think I'd have taken the coward's way out and never gone back there to somehow find the right time to explain properly that my relationship with my other lady really was over this time. End of.

Tearing myself away and promising to ring Lynda very soon, I headed off with poor Stacey nursing a hangover back north to Manchester on Christmas Eve.

As we left, I turned to Stacey and said, 'Do you know summat? I will marry that woman one day.' I just knew it. Deep down in my bones.

I remember it as if it were yesterday. Lynda was such fun to be with. I know I've said it a million times before, but we never argued. We just read each other's minds. It might sound corny, but we were true soulmates in every sense of the word.

Lynda told me later that she felt she'd truly met her match in me. She always believed that you're either a giver or taker in life. She was definitely a giver, but she'd managed in recent years to surround herself with a few takers in her romantic life who'd drained her of energy. In me, she felt she'd found another giver. I like to think that's true. I've never been a penny pincher with money and I think it probably gives you a bit of a clue about my own nature. I like looking after people and, as tough as she could pretend to be as Irene Radford in *The Bill*, the real Lynda Bellingham needed a bit of TLC at the time.

We kept in touch by texting backwards and forwards like two teenagers, as I somehow got through Christmas and New Year without finding the right moment to break the news to my other lady that we couldn't go on.

I'll never forget being out in the bars of Manchester on New Year's Eve and nipping out every quarter of an hour to ring Lynda. Poor bloody girl had slipped in her stockinged feet and fallen down the steep stairs at home after having the cast from *Losing Louis* round for drinks. She'd bruised her back badly and had had to stay in all New Year. I felt desperately sorry for her but couldn't get away to be with her.

On 2 January, I flew back to Spain with the other lady. I still hadn't managed to break the news to her and it was bothering me. I don't like letting people down.

Quite legitimately, I had to fly back to the UK two days later on business and Lynda arranged for her sons' nanny, Alena, to pick me up at Luton airport. We drove to collect Lynda from rehearsals in Hampstead and she was almost bent double with back pain, but it didn't stop us picking up from where we left off on Christmas Eve. I had to fly back to Spain a couple of days later but I was back over the following day. We then had a fantastic time getting to know each other properly.

With the boys back at home, there was no question of me staying at the maisonette. Lynda felt very strongly that she didn't want to get into a relationship, let her boys know about it and then realize she'd made a mistake. She wanted to be certain it was going to be permanent first and I agreed with her 100 per cent.

Nor did she want Nunzio or the press finding out and, to be honest, at that stage, neither did I. For one very good reason: my colourful past which was starting to haunt me.

We began to meet in secret at the Marriott Hotel at Swiss Cottage or the more luxurious Athenaeum in Mayfair. We were very careful at the time never to be seen in public. Everything had to go on behind closed doors.

It was on 8 January 2005, in the Athenaeum, that I knew I'd fallen in love with Lynda hook, line and sinker.

I can tell you the exact moment I realized because I remember it like it was yesterday. Over that life-changing Christmas, there was one cloud on the horizon. Lynda's beloved father Don was dying. He'd had a fall off the back of a trailer whilst cutting trees and had never really recovered. The doctors thought that he'd had a stroke. He'd also been struggling all the while to care for Lynda's mum Ruth, who had Alzheimer's.

She was terribly upset when I saw her. She absolutely thought the world of her dad; they were very close so there were lots of tears. It doesn't take much to set me off at the best of times and as soon as I started trying to comfort her, I was crying as well.

And I knew, I just knew. Right there and then. This wasn't lust; it wasn't a fling. We were both in love. We weren't imagining it. It was the real deal. And that's the way it stayed right up to the end.

Strange how it was a bereavement that brought us together like that. It feels almost as if I've come full circle, and now it's my turn. I can remember Lynda talking about how selfish we are about death and how it is really ourselves we are grieving for. She had strong views on the subject even then, without the slightest idea of what lay ahead for her.

Before such a moment, you like to think you're in love, but in fairness it is very much a sexual thing as well so you can't be entirely certain. But when Lynda started crying and I was comforting her in that hotel bedroom, I knew it without a shadow of a doubt. I'm a very emotional man myself remember.

The following morning, a Sunday, Lynda got up at six

to go down and see her dad and I can honestly say that I didn't think I'd see her again.

She phoned to tell me when he passed away on that very morning, 9 January. She was especially devastated because she hadn't managed to get there on time to be with him at the end. She lost her mum just a matter of weeks afterwards.

I didn't put any pressure on her to see me at the time. I feared that she might have thought it was just a fling between us, and all the while I was praying it wasn't. Then, after her dad's funeral, she phoned to ask if I'd go over to see her. I was there like a shot. Of course I knew I had to tell Lynda the truth about my past at the first opportunity. Before we got in any deeper. Just not now when she had so much on her plate . . .

Reluctantly, I had to go back to Spain where my business was. I couldn't just turn my back on what I'd worked so hard to build up there. It was my livelihood.

I cannot deny it, I was returning a very troubled man. At least my other relationship was now officially over. She'd guessed that I was seeing *the* Lynda Bellingham and asked me straight out. I owned up and, to be fair, she had been quite good about it all. She simply told me to collect my things from her villa, which I did straight away.

But telling Lynda the truth about my past was a big, big deal; a huge deal. I knew that when I next came back it had to come out. I strongly believe that if you put your cards on the table, then everybody knows where they are. I knew there was a good chance I could lose her and by now that was unthinkable. From the minute I boarded that next Monarch plane back to the UK, I was bricking it. I honestly thought I would lose her but I had no other choice but to take that risk and come clean.

It all came out on a long, sleepless Friday night at the Swiss Cottage Marriott, and it was a real heart on the sleeve job. I arrived late, and Lynda was already in bed at the hotel after her evening's performance. I didn't even take off my jacket. I just pulled a bottle of red wine from my cabin bag and explained that there was something she really needed to know about me.

'You may not ever want to see me again after you hear what I have to say Lynda,' I warned, looking at her worried looking face and feeling sick.

Perched at the side of the bed, I took a deep breath and began my long story, while she lay there and listened, absolutely riveted.

I'd already told Lynda bits about my early past, but I started at the beginning and worked my way through it all.

I explained about being fostered by the wonderful Andrews family in Sherborne in Dorset until I was thirteen.

May and Leslie Andrews had brought me up with their own children Doreen, Erenea, Michael and Shaun. I was the youngest and was spoilt rotten, especially by my foster sisters who I love to bits and I'm still in touch with today. May and Leslie are both dead now and I have no contact with Michael. Sadly, Shaun, who moved to New Zealand, died there when I was eighteen.

My real dad, Joe, had always written to me and visited whenever he could, often with his old mate, Freddie. Leslie Andrews moved around a bit with his job in the Ministry of Public Works so I lived in Crewkerne in Somerset, Sherborne in Dorset and Reading in Berkshire, which caused a fair bit of a paperwork hoo-ha for the three separate local authorities.

My old man knew that I was happy with the Andrews and always fought the social workers for me to remain with them. He even offered to pay for me to stay there and I think may have contributed himself after that, but I'm not sure. He never wanted to let me go permanently and be adopted, though. I have huge respect for him for that. He was a lovely guy.

After my father married Marjorie, who had three children of her own, Michael, Carolyn and Lindsay, I went to live with them for a month in the summer holidays when I was thirteen and decided that I wanted to stay there.

When I look back now, it was probably one of the

biggest regrets of my life. Can you imagine how my poor bloody foster mother must have felt? After all she'd done for me? I know now that she was heartbroken but I was too young to properly understand at the time.

I went to the local school until I was fifteen and I joined the army's Junior Leaders, which I thoroughly enjoyed. My dad had been in the Territorial Army and was as proud as hell when I started my real army cadet training at Bramcote Barracks in Nuneaton.

He wasn't quite so proud when I came out a couple of years later.

'Why did you leave?' he wanted to know and I explained. 'You know something, Dad ... You know that guy up the road with the Rolls-Royce and big house? That's what I want and I'm not going to be able to get it in the army.'

He just looked at me and nodded. Years later, at one of Stacey's birthday parties – her third I think – he turned round to me and said, 'You've done it, son.'

Although he was nothing like that himself, he seemed to understand my thirst for more. I worked as a carpet fitter in Crewkerne, met my first wife, Janice, but after a row with her dad, we moved to Cornwall, where I found a job as a roofer.

It was bloody hard graft but you could earn a fortune even in the late seventies. We stayed there for three years before moving back to Crewkerne. We were married when I was twenty-two or twenty-three. I worked all hours and built us a big five-bed house and bought a second-hand Rolls-Royce by the time we had Stacey a few years later.

I also acquired a business partner, Roger Bastable, who's still a friend today, and we opened the Palace nightclub in Crewkerne. Times were good and it was on my way up to John O'Groats in my next Rolls-Royce which was canary yellow (you can imagine how Lynda laughed at that bit) that we stopped off at Blackpool to see the illuminations. It was teeming with people and it struck me what a great place it would be to open another nightclub.

Stacey was only a few months old when we sold up in Crewkerne and moved up to Blackpool. I wasn't wrong; it was a bloody gold mine. But it didn't last. After the miners' strike and the recession, money became scarce in the north. Interest rates were sky high and I lost everything.

I've always hated winter and loved the sunshine so, taking a chance, I moved Janice and Stacey out to Florida, where Bradley was born, to open another nightclub. It didn't work out and we moved back to the UK before Brad started school.

Living just outside Chelmsford, I started fishing around for new business and met a couple of finance guys dealing in high yield investment schemes. I was intrigued. God knows where I got my confidence from because it sure as hell wasn't from my dad, but knowing nothing about finance, I set up my own trading company with Janice as a co-director.

Somewhere along the way, I was introduced to a man who knew a man who knew an American man and we moved back to Florida. All was going well until one day in 1997 the FBI knocked on my door . . .

I swear I didn't realize I'd done anything wrong. I thought I had nothing to hide. Unfortunately the FBI didn't see it that way. Apparently, I was accused of being reckless with other people's money because of the particular wording in a contract. When I arrived back at Gatwick, two plain clothes policemen were waiting to arrest me at passport control.

To save my wife going to prison, I pleaded guilty at Southwark Crown Court to furnishing false or misleading information that didn't comply with some part of some finance act. As a director, Janice too was liable, but if we both went to prison, who would look after the children? I couldn't risk them being taken into care, so I was prepared to take the rap and let Janice plead not guilty.

To everybody's shock – including my lawyers and one of the arresting officers in the case, who Lynda got to know much later – I was sentenced to twenty-one months and headed for HMP Brixton.

It's always been my nature to put my head down when

necessary – to sit at the back rather than at the forefront of things, because I'd rather watch what's going on. That's what I did inside and I managed to survive the nine months of my sentence that I actually served. Thankfully, it wasn't all at Brixton.

Determined not to look back, I put it behind me when I came out a free man. I opened a pub in Aldbourne, near Marlborough, with Janice as the licensee, until my marriage broke up less than two years later.

Lynda listened intently as I told her everything about my past. I knew that if I left anything out, I could be as sure as hell that it would come back and bite me on the bum.

God knows how many glasses of wine we drank in those six hours as she sat there, fascinated by my story, butting in only occasionally to egg me on asking for more. The real questions came later.

When I'd eventually finished, I looked up and said, 'Right, I'll be off . . .'

'Why?' she asked.

'After what I've just told you, you don't really want to know me . . .' I shrugged, fully expecting her to turn round and tell me to go. After all, Lynda did have a very public image as well as two children to think of.

But she swore first, then kissed me and said, 'Don't be ridiculous! I don't care what you did. It's in the past. Let's forget about it and get on with the present.'

Being me, I just burst out crying. As I keep saying, I am a very emotional man!

Between tears, I told her to think seriously about what I'd said and that I'd understand if she didn't want to see me again. 'You're the one that has to face your friends, the press and the public.'

But she would have none of it, and I cannot put into the words the relief that I felt. This phenomenal woman wasn't going to fire me off after all. She believed me and she was giving me a chance, us a chance. I sure as hell wasn't going to blow it.

Afterwards the questions started. She asked millions and millions of questions for months and months. She was intrigued by my story. She kept saying that it would make a great movie! She always wanted to write the screenplay herself and cast Ray Winstone to play me.

Who knows, maybe if time hadn't run out on her, she'd have done just that.

I was never looking for any kind of recognition, though. Not one bit. I didn't want to be famous or even infamous (which was probably more likely given my past). At the end of the day, I loved the woman, not her fame. I would have been quite happy for Lynda to pack her bags and come and live with me in Spain, where I'd take care of her. And she seriously thought about it, before it became apparent that her acting career was about to take off again.

Just as long as we were both happy ... That was all that mattered to me, and after her reaction to what I'd just told her, there didn't seem to be any reason at all why we couldn't be. Well, for the next ten years at least.

CHAPTER 4

ALWAYS THE LITTLE THINGS

......

At the back of the glove compartment in the Range Rover, there's a half-full bag of children's sticky jelly sweets. Colin the Caterpillar, they're called, from M&S, and one of Lynda's favourite treats for long car journeys.

I'll never eat them because I don't really have a sweet tooth and, besides, I try not to snack between meals. It's almost springtime when I find them and I know I can't throw them away. At least not yet. Not until I'm good and ready.

I can see Lynda now, sneaking one onto the inside of my left leg as I'm driving down the motorway. 'Go on, you know, you want to . . .' she'd tease in that vamped up, sexy voice she could put on. It was as natural and easy to her as turning a tap on.

More often than not I'd protest, then give in. No matter how many times she pulled the same trick, it always made me laugh. Then we'd both laugh. She had the dirtiest laugh I've ever heard on a woman. It was like her sense of humour: irresistible.

So when I first found them, it gave me a real jolt, pang, or whatever you want to call it. A bloody half-eaten bag of jelly sweets that are probably well past their sell-by date by now actually made me cry. I ask you!

You expect it with clothes, shoes and all the personal stuff that's still taking up space at home.I know I'll have to get rid of it all in the end, but I don't want to do anything too rash right now. Maybe I'll auction some for charity when I decide. Funny, I'm not usually a hoarder.

God knows what Lynda would think. She loved shopping for a bargain but she'd always team it up with a designer piece. She wasn't against foraging in charity shops either. A couple of years before she died, we were in Brighton visiting her late sister Barbara's husband David and she spotted a Harris tweed jacket in a window for twenty-five quid. I love Harris tweed. She practically shoved me through the door and forced my arms into the jacket before it was dragged back off me and folded up into a used carrier bag. Next stop the dry cleaners!

But Lynda was never a hoarder – often to the delight of her family and friends, especially Stacey who's been grateful more than once for an Armani or a Michael Kors cast off. Whenever she'd finished with something – clothes, hand-bags, shoes – Lynda would hand it on to a good home or the charity shop. I remember one year not that long back she donated a beautiful winter coat to the Age UK charity winter appeal to keep old people warm.

Sometimes she hadn't even finished with stuff but if she knew somebody close had admired something she had, she'd pass it on anyway. That was Lynda. Kind, generous and always putting other people before herself. I used to tell people: Lynda thinks about one person and one person only, and that's Everybody Else.

Before she died, she gave some of her really nice stuff away to close family and friends. Knowing that she didn't have long left, she actually went through her wardrobe and put stickers with names on the things she wanted some-body in particular to have. I swear she almost enjoyed deciding who would suit what the best.

Without a thought for herself, Lynda carried on organiz-ing everything and everybody right up to the very end. I think it was the ex-*EastEnders* actress and *Loose Women* panellist Nadia Sawalha who said after she died: 'That woman could juggle plates like nothing you've ever seen.' And she wasn't wrong there. The two went back a long way because Lynda had helped Nadia land her first part in showbiz, playing the son's girlfriend in the Oxo adverts.

Despite her own cull, there's still plenty of Lynda's stuff lying all around the apartment. Everything is still exactly as she left it. Her twenty or so brightly coloured cashmere jumpers are still individually wrapped in tissue paper in drawers, and even her two dressing gowns – a white one and a grey and white one that she bought on a honeymoon stopover in Antigua – are still hanging on a hook on our en-suite bathroom door. It's painful to see and yet strangely comforting at the same time.

I've learnt that with this bereavement game that there are no rules. None at all. One minute you're OK and getting there; the next you're in bits. Up and down like a fiddler's elbow and it's always the little things that really set you off. Always. Usually it's when you least expect them. Just like rifling through the glove compartment in the car for my sunglasses and finding a few bloody children's sweets that completely floor you.

It's the memories, of course, that these daft things bring racing back. They're always there in your mind but moments like this make them real again. It's hard to explain but suddenly you're right back there. The memories aren't in the past any more; they're real and happening all over again. I wish.

Touring with Lynda when she was on the road with

Calendar Girls, in panto, or in her daytime TV series *My Tasty Travels* and *Country House Sunday*, could be hard going. Don't get me wrong; it was great fun as well. It got us out of London and seeing a bit more of the country, which we both loved doing for a start. It suited our gypsy spirits, Lynda would joke. Occasionally we'd go by train if she was doing a charity event in the north (she once even bought herself a senior railcard because it meant she could travel first class from Leeds to London for £45!). Ninety-nine times out of a hundred, though, I'd drive her in the Range Rover, which was always absolutely packed to the gunnels with clothes, shoes, toiletries – hers and mine! She would 'navigate', regularly arguing with the satnav as she chewed on her sweets for most of the journey. She hated the M1 and M25 with a vengeance; she never felt safe on them and always asked me to go down the M40 if we could because it wasn't as busy.

If she'd just come off stage on a Saturday night, Lynda would be hyper and exhausted at the same time when we were heading back either to London or on the next leg of the tour. Often we'd give her *Calendar Girls* co-stars Jan Harvey and Siân Phillips a lift back to London from wherever we happened to be: Manchester, Leeds, Llandudno. Oh we saw the world! The world of British theatre, that is. Sometimes I'd be the only one awake. Just as well when I was the one behind the wheel . . .

We spent hours in the car together in those days. We might have the radio on but it wouldn't be loud so we could chat. Lynda had an opinion on everything and she was never afraid to air it wherever she was and whoever she was with. Once she even told Prince Charles that his PRIME (The Prince's Initiative for Mature Enterprise) organization needed to be sexier. She was an ambassador for it and I think she was using advertising speak to talk about its image.

Happy days. The main reason I tagged along on these tours was so that we could always be together. We'd never have seen each other otherwise and I don't think either of us could have coped with long periods apart. We just loved being together. When we arrived wherever we were going, we'd check in to a hotel, check out the beds and sometimes, if there was a pool, we'd have a swim.

Lynda would go on stage and do her thing and I'd run my property business from various dressing rooms, hotel bars and bedrooms. Thank God for mobile phones and laptops. How did we ever live without them?

By now of course I was officially her Mr Spain.

The nickname originally came from the actress Alison Steadman, who was appearing in *Losing Louis* with Lynda right at the start of our relationship. The two of them were in the dressing room chatting one day and it was getting confusing when Lynda talked about 'Michael'. Alison never knew whether she meant me or her son Michael. Even her old Oxo husband had been a Michael. So one day she asked if 'Mr Spain' was coming for the weekend.

That was it! Lynda loved the nickname and it stuck, becoming popular when she used it to talk about me on *Loose Women*, which she joined in 2007 after Denise Welch put in a good word for her – the two of them had found themselves riding a tandem together at a charity event. Although Lynda didn't know Denise that well, she had a lot of respect for her as an actress. They'd been on the *Loose Women* set together once before when Lynda had been promoting her play *Vincent River*.

People still come up to me now in the street to ask if I am Mr Spain. Lynda used to joke that I'd become a celebrity in my own right. Never my ambition, though, B!

After the big confession night at the Swiss Cottage Marriott, we'd slipped into a happy, loving routine.

During the week, Lynda usually had to sort the boys out. The only time she had free was from the end of Saturday night's performance until the Monday evening performance. She always went back home to cook Michael and Robbie Sunday lunch, then she'd nip out in the afternoon to meet me at the hotel.

There was no way in those early days that I was going to

turn my back on the business and the income I'd built up in Spain, so I began to come over to the UK as often as I could at weekends. It wasn't just that our sex life was incredible, which it was without a shadow of a doubt. Until she became seriously ill with cancer, me and Lynda made love every single day. If you truly love someone that's what naturally happens. (In case I get accused of being not very gentlemanly here, I'd like to point out that I'm not saying anything Lynda hasn't said before or that she'd want keeping quiet. She was one of the *Loose Women*, remember!)

But although that was an important part of our relationship for both of us, it was so much more than just sex. I always tell people how we never argued in all the time we were together because I am proud of it. We clicked from the start and stayed on the same wavelength. We didn't need to argue. How many couples can honestly and truthfully say that?

But being a stickler for detail, Lynda would remind me there was actually one bit of a tiff very early on. I always said that it didn't count because we weren't officially a couple back then.

It only happened because I booked flights backwards and forwards from Spain to the UK for weekends in advance without consulting Lynda, and she was panicking about the speed things were going. It was something and nothing that blew over almost as soon as it started. Like me,

Lynda was nervous because she'd had her own fingers burnt in her previous marriage.

After I'd come clean and told her my life story, Lynda told me hers. How she'd been adopted by Ruth and Don and all the insecurities that caused no matter how much they'd loved her. She told me, also, about tracking down her birth mother Marjorie to Canada after Robbie was born.

Though neither of us knew it at the time, worse was to come for Lynda when Marjorie died in February 2012. At ninety-four, she was much older than poor Lynda had been when she died; so much for genetics. Nobody in the family had the decency to inform Lynda in time so that she could attend the funeral. She was eventually told in an email that I opened on my phone when she was appearing in *Calendar Girls*. I can't remember exactly where we were but I think it was somewhere in Yorkshire. It was early morning and we were lying in bed; Lynda was still fast asleep. I waited for her to wake up before I broke the news by saying: 'Your mum has passed over.'

She seemed puzzled. 'That's not the normal way you would talk, Michael,' she said and she was right. I wouldn't normally have used the words 'passed over' but I didn't know what else to say. There was no easy way to come out with this one. So I'd just read out the contents of the email.

It was a huge shock to her. Huge. It wasn't so much the fact that Marjorie had died but more that she was dead and buried before Lynda was told. A couple of years before that there'd been a fuss over who had paid for some flights while we were trying to get Marjorie, who had Alzheimer's, and her sister Shirley into good care homes. Somebody in the family or the church they belonged to had read somewhere about my past and jumped to a very wrong conclusion. Lynda was really upset then as she was now.

Going to her birth mother's funeral was something she'd wanted to do. I think she simply wanted to be finally recognized as Marjorie's daughter. It's perfectly natural, isn't it? Yet here she was finding out by bloody email. They couldn't even take the trouble to pick up a phone.

The thing about Lynda is that whenever she cried, her whole face would swell up completely. I've never seen anything like it. That day she had to be on stage in a few hours' time so she was trying desperately to hold back the tears. I felt so sorry for her all over again, as well as angry at Marjorie's family for not accepting Lynda because she was illegitimate.

Having been born out of wedlock, she was a shameful secret right to the very end for the strict churchgoing family. It upset her terribly for a long time. She used to say it was like being rejected all over again, especially when she later received a solicitor's letter asking if she wanted to put in a financial bid for her mother's engagement ring from the estate. They actually wanted her to bloody buy it! Lynda and the boys were Marjorie's closest blood relatives. Her only daughter and two only grandchildren. Lynda didn't want her money or her diamonds, just some sort of loving recognition. Was it really too much to ask?

I could understand how she felt because of the situation with my own birth mother. You never really get over that feeling of rejection, I don't think. Perhaps that's what drove us both to work so hard and achieve. We had to keep proving ourselves. But who really knows?

Years ago when I was in my thirties, when I had the Palace nightclub, I tracked down my own mother. I'd got chatting to one of my part-time doormen (or as I preferred to call him, an eviction technician!) who was also a tax inspector and I mentioned that I wouldn't mind tracing my mother. I told him what information I had and the following week he said that he'd found the guy who'd witnessed her third wedding (after my dad divorced her).

The witness was living on the Isle of Wight so I headed off there that weekend. Going straight to the local library, I trawled laboriously through the electoral roll, which wasn't computerized in those days. Bugger me if I didn't manage to find him.

I'll never forget pulling up outside his old house in my naff yellow Roller – it was bought in the 'loadsamoney'

1980s, remember; people were flash down south – the next day and getting the poor woman who lived there all excited.

'I've won the *Sun* Bingo!' she yelled. After calming her down and explaining that I was sorry but I wasn't there to deliver a big cheque, I told her that I was looking for somebody. Her husband was an ex-copper, now working as a taxi driver, and he found me an address. Eventually I was standing in High Wycombe on my birth mother's doorstep.

I'd been in two minds as to whether to actually knock when it came to it, but curiosity got the better of me and I banged on the door. A dark-haired guy in glasses who was probably around the age I am now answered, and I explained who I was looking for but not why. He had a handful of beers in his hand and he told me that was his wife and led me into the back garden.

She took one look at me and said, 'Oh my god. It's my Michael, isn't it?' Her poor husband nearly had a heart attack and dropped the cans of beer. Can you imagine the shock? He knew nothing about me. He disappeared for a walk with the dog and me and my mother sat outside talking. When it turned cold we went inside the flat, where we continued to talk for another hour.

I'd like to say the story had a happy ending but, in truth, apart from an odd phone call, I never saw her again after that Sunday. There'd been no emotional bond there at all. Nothing. Perhaps I'd been coloured by what my dad had told me about my mother, but I felt nothing like I felt with for him and my stepmother or my wonderful foster family. She was a stranger to me. All I can say is that finding her had laid some skeletons buried somewhere deep inside me to rest. The old nature versus nurture argument is an interesting one in my case, I guess. Like I said earlier, psychologists really could have a field day . . .

If me and Lynda had needed another common bond to strengthen our own relationship, I guess this was one. After being separated from our genetic mothers as babies, we'd both loved and treasured our own families to bits. We talked openly to each other about how our pasts had affected us and it was why we liked to support the Barnardo's charity. Lynda had done so very quietly for more than twenty years, until she was ready to tell people about her own adoption when her first memoir, *Lost and Found,* came out in 2011.

At her memorial, the charity's Serena Greaves described Lynda as a truly wonderful lady who always had time for everybody and was an absolute joy to work with.

Serena told the story of how, when Lynda was once performing in Scarborough, she met a group of young homeless people and gave them a fantastic afternoon that included a personal tour of the theatre and free tickets for a performance.

'She had a wonderful way of putting people at ease and was genuinely interested in what people had to say and their personal stories. She always gave 110 per cent to everything. I've seen her fit three engagements in for us on one day while on tour. Throughout, she was always professional.'

Yep, that was Lynda. She understood, which was why she was always so hardworking and caring, doing whatever she could to help others. She never forgot, either, that if it hadn't been for Ruth and Don, her own life could have taken a very different course. She was eternally grateful to them.

Unlike Lynda, I had been fortunate enough to know my real and very loving father Joe, who died in my arms of prostate cancer just after his eightieth birthday on 7 December 2010. Sometimes, seeing Lynda so ill with cancer was like seeing my dad all over again. It brought it all back. Now they're lying a couple of feet away from each other in Townsend Cemetery, Crewkerne. One day I'll be lying there with them both. It's not something I can, in all fairness, say that I dread.

The bizarre thing about seeing somebody you really love die is that it takes away your own fear of dying, or at least it has done in my case. I don't fear death at all any more. If

I went now, it wouldn't bother me two hoots because I know I'll meet up with Lynda again when that day comes. On the one hand I can't wait, but on the other I really don't want to go just yet. I've got too much to do and, besides, I have the boys and Stacey and my grandsons to look after.

I promised Lynda that I would always look after Robbie and Michael. She hated leaving them without a mother at thirty-one and twenty-six, without seeing them properly established in their lives with homes and wives of their own. She prepared them as much as she could. But, in the end, I don't know if anything really can.

I have to say that Lynda was probably one of the most loving mothers I have ever seen. When Bradley came back from Florida to live with us at the age of eighteen or nineteen, she treated him like her own son. And because she has no daughter of her own, she and Stacey were always close.

Stacey used to say that she felt quite guilty when she came over for dinner, especially on Christmas Day, and Lynda wouldn't let her help in the kitchen. She'd spend all morning cooking and whenever Stacey tried to help, she'd say 'Sit down Stacey', and you couldn't argue with her. Lynda wouldn't let anybody do anything. She was the hostess and like everything else she carried it off to perfection. Absolute perfection.

Stacey says she used to love the moment when Lynda had done absolutely everything that needed doing and she finally sat down to join everyone. She'd look round the big glass dining table, see everybody smiling and then she'd be happy. She'd relax and enjoy being surrounded by her family. Lynda loved that.

For years, of course, there was always tension round the family dinner table for her when she was married to Nunzio. All the while, she was being portrayed in the Oxo adverts as having the perfect family life.

I could not get my head round all this when Lynda first told me about the problems then, and in her first, short marriage to the *Confessions* films producer, Greg Smith, which was never consummated. I kept thinking, *Why would anybody want to hurt or abuse – or not make love to – this funny, kind, beautiful lady?* I can't get my head round it even to this day. I find it really hard.

Greg Smith is dead and I've never met Nunzio socially, and I never want to. I know that he is Michael and Robbie's father, but there was absolutely no way I would have let him come to the funeral if he'd asked. Not in a million years.

Hearing about Lynda's past made me all the more determined to protect and care for her from the very start of our relationship, even though some of her famous friends were a little bit wary of me, to say the least. I just hope I managed to prove them wrong in the ten fantastically happy years that me and Lynda were together.

One of the first friends we both had reason to be grateful to was Pat Hay, who I'd already met of course. Our secret affair in hotel rooms might have been exciting but it was also proving expensive. Luckily Pat, who is a make-up artist, was going to Cornwall to film *Doc Martin* during our first summer together, and she was kind enough to let us use her place just round the corner from Lynda's. Good old Pat. She misses Lynda terribly. We all do.

I first met the boys and her sisters Jean and Barbara, and their husbands on Easter Sunday 2005. Lynda felt it was time that we met but, for her sake, I was still a little unsure. I was still very protective of her and aware of the damage that my past might do.

Lynda went ahead, though, and organized a big dinner round at her place. She'd made a real effort. She always did. It was always the full works when she was entertaining. A three-course meal with the best china and glasses for this and glasses for that. But the occasion didn't get off to the best of starts. Lynda had told her family that I'd been to prison and it all felt a bit cold and strained. More than a bit, in fact. Let's just say that nobody exactly welcomed me into the family with open arms that day.

Thinking about it now, before I was one of those men I'd probably have reacted the same way if Stacey had told me she was seeing a man who'd been inside,. Today, though, I wouldn't be quite so judgemental, I'd want to know what he'd been in for before I made my mind up about him.

Apart from immediate family, not many people knew about us at all. We kept it very quiet. Poor Lynda was leading a double life for a long time. With hindsight I suppose you could say it was good practice for keeping a secret, which was to come in handy after she'd been diagnosed with cancer.

After August 2005 we didn't need to bother hiding away any more. Our secret was out when a Sunday tabloid photographer papped us late one Friday night at Langan's Brasserie. My flight was delayed so I didn't arrive until after midnight to meet Lynda, her accountant and a couple of his American clients. It was a lovely summer night and they were all sitting round a huge circular table right in the centre of the restaurant. It was well known that if you got that table, you had to be somebody.

As I walked in, my trolley case clinking with wine bottles I'd brought over from Spain, I was chatting to the maître d' when Lynda came running up, flung her arms round me and physically stuck her tongue down my throat. That was my girl!

Whoa! I thought. We'd always been so careful not to be caught in public.

'I don't care any more, Michael, I love you,' she whispered. Of course when we finally walked out of the place, a photographer was lying in wait for us, flash at the ready.

We stayed at the Athenaeum that night and when I asked Lynda next day if she had any regrets about us being caught, she replied, 'No. I planned it!' Devious lady! This was her way of getting it out in the open. Over and done with. As soon as.

It was the *Sunday People* that ran the photograph and story with the headline about me being wanted by the FBI. The other papers followed it up the next day. The *Daily Mail* had a right old go at me. Oh dear. Just as well the honest streak that had been passed on to me from my old dad had made me confess everything to Lynda so early on. Otherwise it could have been a very different story. I always knew my past would catch up with me if I didn't come clean and I was right. Now, though, I was worried about it affecting Lynda. She didn't need any more problems in her life just when everything between us was going so well.

She'd recently lost both her parents, within weeks of each other, and she still hadn't managed to shake off a troublesome ex-husband. This was the last thing she needed. I can't prove it but, even now, I think she probably lost work because she was married to me; an ex crim. I still feel guilty about it.

Typical Lynda, she took it all on the chin. Her argument was: 'You haven't killed anybody; you haven't robbed a little old lady. The people you were dealing with were multi-millionaires and you've done your time.' End of story.

If it had been any different she would have kicked me out there and then; I'd have been gone.

The one question people who didn't know her always ask me today is: 'Was Lynda really as nice as she seemed?' I always tell them, 'Yes, absolutely.' That's probably not strictly true. She was much nicer. She was no fool, either. If you crossed her, that was it; you would be cut out. No problem. She would not go back, but for that to happen you would have had to have taken her right to the limit.

In a way, Lynda's niceness was almost a fault because – what's the expression? – kindness can show weakness? It made her vulnerable and open to being taken advantage of, hence her previous marriages. So I can see why her family and friends might have been a bit wary of me.

There had been no rush for me to be introduced to her friends until after the story of our relationship came out in the papers. After that happened I met two of her oldest actor mates, Biggins and Nickolas Grace, for an awkward lunch at The Wolseley in Mayfair.

Biggins's first words to me were: 'I hear you've been a naughty boy,' followed by 'Do you have your own property?' and 'Are you after Lynda's money?'

I thought it was a bit smug of him, to say the least, but I gave back as good as I got by telling him the answers were yes, yes and no, absolutely not. I then told him what I was earning, pointing out that it was probably more than he was!

I don't think they knew how to take me, and it's fair to say that I didn't I hit it off with anybody at first because everybody was busy sussing me out. I'm not going to say they were unfriendly, but they were not exactly open and welcoming either, if that makes sense. I could see what was going through their minds: *Why is Lynda Bellingham with a man from Somerset who's been in prison when she could have her pick of any man going?* To be honest, it's a fair enough question, and I've come to respect her friends for not wanting to let anyone else walk all over her.

If I remember rightly, we all left The Wolseley that night on fairly reasonable, if not exactly the best, terms. I think I even paid the restaurant bill just to prove a point!

*

By now, me and Lynda had been together long enough to know that our feelings for each other were every bit as strong as they had been when we started this relationship. If not more so. It still wasn't the right time for me to move in with the boys, though, so Lynda decided to invest in The Love Nest – a little one bed flat in East Finchley.

She'd always been conscious that she had no pension (neither do I, but I've always believed in property before pensions; still do) and bought it as an investment for her old age. Wishful thinking. I chipped in with the costs. I loved that place; our first sort-of-proper home together. Lynda did too, especially when she realized she had 'a man who can'. I may not be able to stand on stage and act, or cook up a cordon bleu dinner, but I can turn my hand to any plumbing, decorating or joinery work. I could build a house blindfolded, no problem. Brad takes after me in that respect; he's doing very nicely with his loft conversion business. Chip off the old block.

Eventually we did a swap. Michael moved in to the flat and we moved into Lynda's bigger maisonette with Robbie. I closed my office in Spain two years after we got married so that I could concentrate on launching my online estate agency and be London-based. We bought our first real home together in a luxury converted psychiatric hospital in May 2006. Bradley joined us there the following year and, in February 2008, we moved into a bigger four-bed apartment in the same complex. It wasn't the plan, but it turned out to be Lynda's last home.

The first real testing time in our relationship came when I decided to stop drinking. It was 2006 and I'd just registered with a GP in East Finchley. Living in Spain, I hadn't seen a doctor for a good few years so he did the usual routine tests and then called me back in.

'Michael, you're a very fit man, but if you continue drinking as you are doing, you'll probably have a stroke in ten years' time,' he warned.

He frightened the life out of me. I'd only just met Lynda and I really didn't want to fuck it all up. I knew that in the first throes of love we'd been drinking far too much red wine. I am naturally a man of extremes so it was all or nothing with me. One of anything was never enough, and Lynda was the same.

Most people enjoy a social drink, but in Spain, I have to admit, it had become a bit too much of a habit. It was a way of life out there with us expats, many of whom didn't have anything much better to do all day. As it helped to oil the wheels of business, drinking crept into my work life as well as my social life. And I am not the sort of person to stop after a couple of beers, so I could see it was becoming a problem.

The thing about drinking is that it soon becomes a habit if you're not careful, and I have to admit that it became that again for me after Lynda died. In my defence, all I can really say is that at that time I needed it to relax me and help me sleep.

It's not just the grief that's hard to cope with, it's the sheer bloody loneliness as well. Overwhelming. I don't have the sort of job where I go into an office from 9 a.m. till 5 p.m. every day, so I can end up spending whole days and nights on my own if I'm not careful. And I can tell you it's not much fun. I keep saying it but the trick is to keep busy. You gotta keep busy. On the go.

Once I've made up my mind to do something, I go for it and that's what happened. When I walked out of the doctor's surgery, I didn't touch a drop for the next seven years, apart from a glass of champagne on the day we got engaged. We didn't even indulge at our wedding, even though I stopped the champagne flowing when the bar bill reached thirty grand. Yes, really! Thirsty lot, these celebrities!

Lynda was waiting for me when I came out of the surgery and looked amazed when I told her what the GP had said and what I'd decided to do. She didn't say so right there and then, but I know she didn't believe I could do it. She hadn't yet clocked what a stubborn bastard I can be!

The other thing with drink is that not having one isn't a problem once you've made the decision and adjusted to the change, but only as long as you're in the company of other sober people. And very often I wasn't . . .

Lynda always said that I gave her an ultimatum the following year: either she gave up drink or it was over between us. I don't remember it quite that way. But I had had a belly full of boozy lunches and dinners with her famous friends. Like us, they were usually people of extremes themselves. So, when I was watching them knock it back for hours on end, and listening to them getting louder and louder, as I sipped my sparkling water and lime, it was irritating to say the least. As well as boring. You have no time for it when you're not doing it yourself. We didn't argue about it, but I told Lynda how I felt and she even agreed with me really. She just never did anything about it at first.

Things eventually came to a head a good year later. I'd undergone some more tests and been given a clean bill of health by the doctor. I felt much better and looked it as well. I was as fit as a fiddle and had bags of energy.

We'd been to a lunchtime do one Sunday, at the actress Amanda Redman's house, when I finally had enough. Lynda had been drinking red wine all afternoon, finishing off with a huge brandy or two, and I knew she was plastered as I drove her back home to north London. When we got in, I warned her not to do what she usually did when she was like this. Normally she'd go into the kitchen, pick up the phone, ring her friends and talk to them for hours on end while I sat in the lounge watching TV on my own like a lemon. I'd go to bed and be fast asleep when she eventually climbed in. Next morning she wouldn't even remember who she'd phoned. Of course she did the same again that evening.

I know it went back to the days of her second marriage when she didn't see much of her friends and would catch up with them by phone. But she had me now and I was getting a bit of fed up of this happening. It wasn't every weekend or anything like that. More often when a TV friend had finished a series. Sometimes, though, it could be one after the other for a month. I'd tried to talk to Lynda about it and warned her that if she wanted to carry on like this, I wouldn't bother coming over to see her at weekends. I'd just come in the week when she was sober. But it didn't seem to be registering.

We hadn't been back long from Amanda's when we got a phone call from Lynda's sister Barbara in Aylesbury to say their sister Jean had been mugged outside her London home and was lying in a pool of blood in Coleridge Road, Crouch End. A passer-by had called her from Jean's phone I think. Lynda was in no fit state to do anything about it, so I headed over there alone to take Jean to the Whittington Hospital, where she was treated for a broken arm. When I got back, Lynda was still slumped in the chair where I'd left her hours earlier.

Knowing we couldn't go on like this, I had a difficult decision to make. On the one hand I didn't want to lose Lynda. And I really didn't want to lose her. But on the other hand, we weren't going anywhere if she was going to carry on drinking like this when I wasn't.

I didn't just intend to give her a short, sharp shock when I got up at 4 a.m. the next morning to catch an early flight back to Spain; I was genuinely mad with her. Lynda thought the world of me (from what she'd kept telling me) and her family. Yet here she was putting everything in jeopardy. And for what?

Other than the odd puff in my youth, I've never been a smoker myself but Lynda had been, and she'd managed to stop long before she met me when she returned from filming in Russia. I was praying she'd be able to do the same with alcohol.

Lynda's family and extended family really did mean everything to her and she'd do anything for any of us. Anything. All the problems with Nunzio, her birth mother and the lack of a genetic father had made her value us all the more I guess.

It wasn't an ultimatum: I wasn't asking her to stop drinking altogether. I just wanted her to cut back when I was around. It really was up to her.

CHAPTER 5

A HEAVY WEIGHT ON
MY SHOULDERS

......

It's early in the morning on 16 April and almost six months to the day since Lynda died. I am standing in the bathroom at my friends Barry and Rose Cox's house, staring at my reflection in the mirror above the sink.

I notice it straight away. The right-hand side of the collar of my suit jacket has a thick, deep crease running right across it. And I know I'm wearing the wrong suit.

I'd grabbed a dry cleaner's plastic suit carrier from the wardrobe that I could see contained a black suit. In my rush to get on the M25 down to Somerset before 6 a.m., when the traffic starts to build up, I'd shoved it in the boot of the Range Rover without properly checking that it was mine.

What I've actually done is pick up Lynda son Michael's almost identical suit. How do I know? Because when we carried Lynda's mahogany coffin in and out of church at her funeral, five months earlier, he balanced it on his right shoulder; I balanced it on my left. And, just in case I'd forgotten how heavy and solid it was, that crease is there to remind me. All over again.

Everybody said today would be hard, going back to St Bartholomew's Parish Church in Crewkerne for another funeral, my first there since Lynda's. Be prepared, they warned, it'll really hit you. And I thought I was prepared. Until this moment when I am getting changed after a long journey. A bit like when I lost Lynda really.

Already I'm in bits. And I haven't even seen the coffin yet or heard the first hymn. I'd expected to shed a few tears in church, of course. Well okay, more than a few to be fair, but I had my hankie at the ready in my pocket. All week I've been telling myself that this funeral is going to be very different to Lynda's. I'm not as emotionally involved for a start. I am paying my respects to an old friend and neighbour of my 89-year-old stepmum. I don't know how old Coral actually was but I'm guessing she'd be a similar age. A lot older than Lynda, anyway. I'm not saying it's not still hard on her family and loved ones who are left behind. Really hard. I learnt that from my dad's death. Coral was a lovely lady and any loss is a loss when it's someone you love.

My mum will miss her for a start. She'd been looking forward to Coral moving into the same nursing home as her. It's just that, to me right now, it seems more, well, fair I suppose, when somebody goes at a good old age. In the same way that it can never, ever, be right for parents to bury their own children.

Of course I should have realized that it wasn't my black suit, which was just like the one I'd bought Michael. They'd both been bought off the peg but we'd had them professionally altered for Lynda's funeral. There was no way in the world we were going to let her down and not look smart; we had to do her proud. We owed it to her. Brad and Robbie already had black suits. When I look closely I can tell that this one is that bit too long for me for a start. But because I'd fitted into it so easily, it hadn't clicked until I'd looked in the mirror.

Since Lynda hasn't been here to feed me up, I've lost almost two stone, going down from around 13.5 to 11.5 stone, so I can easily fit into Michael's 32-inch trousers and smaller jacket. I've always been a size up from him, even though we're a similar height.

What's the saying again: be careful what you wish for? When me and Lynda had actually tried to lose weight, it was always such a struggle, especially when we were on tour without proper cooking facilities. Hotel breakfasts, dinner out every night and M&S snacks in between (especially

Lynda's favourite mini-mince pies with a blob of cream if it was Christmas time) didn't do either of our waistlines any favours.

Being in the public eye and on camera, which automatically adds ten pounds, Lynda was always conscious of her weight. Probably never more so than when she was in *Calendar Girls*, where she had to strip off, and on *Strictly Come Dancing*, which incidentally she hated doing – on telly she always used to think she looked really hefty when in reality it was only because she was standing next to the tiny professional dancers. She never watched the show after her series. For years after, she said she always felt so sick that it made her stomach churn whenever she heard the opening music to it.

The only time I'd seen Lynda really big though was in *The Romanovs* and that was a long time before we met. Watching the DVD together years later, I hardly recognized her. She told me that she'd been comfort eating throughout the filming in Russia because she was away from the boys. When she came back, she was the heaviest she'd ever been at 14 stone but she immediately set to work to lose it all again by dieting and hiring a personal fitness trainer to get herself back into shape.

Lynda always used to say she'd never had much confidence about her body. God knows why. I always loved her just as she was. Perhaps that was why she was so perfect as fat nurse Hilda Price in *General Hospital*. She landed the part in 1972 after leaving drama school and was always proud that she'd been in the nation's first daytime soap, which paved the way for more TV work including *Doctor on the Go*, *The Sweeney*, *Yes, Honestly* and *Within These Walls*. By then she was a household name.

Full of stories, she used to make people laugh with the one about how, for six months, she had to sweat it out in a padded suit that stretched from her neck to the top of her thighs filming *General Hospital*. Then Hilda, her character, lost weight after winning a competition to go to a health farm. Lynda was able to take the suit off and was immediately inundated with letters from viewers wanting to know her diet secret! If only it was that easy in real life, she used to say.

Lynda loved good food; both cooking it and eating it. As she got older, she used to moan about not being able to eat as much as she used to do without piling on the pounds.

I don't know much about women's hormones but she cursed them. Well, I say I don't know much about them, but I knew when her next HRT injection was due! She used to have them every six months and it was always obvious when the effect was wearing off. She didn't get grumpy; Lynda was never grumpy. But she did get stressed about little things that she wouldn't normally bother about. If we were driving somewhere, for instance, she'd be worrying about whether we'd get a parking space before we'd even arrived. I'd ask when her next injection was due and she'd check her diary to find it was coming up in a couple of weeks' time.

Relieved, she'd say, 'You're right again Michael.'

When the cancer really took a grip, of course, she couldn't eat very much anyway. Everything tasted strange and her mouth could be full of painful ulcers. A few months ago, I caught a weird virus and one of the symptoms was that my mouth was full of ulcers. I realized then just what she'd been through.

Not able to physically eat, let alone digest, all her favourite grub, the weight dropped off her. At the end she was just skin and bone; especially her legs. The irony wasn't lost on her. At one time she'd have given anything to be skinny without trying. Or so she'd thought. But that was BC. Before Cancer. Before both our lives changed forever. A whole bloody lifetime ago. Literally.

It's the same with me. I've cursed the first signs of a middle-aged paunch on myself before now. Too many times to count I've cut out the carbs again and stepped up the number of morning sit-ups.

Yet the reason I'm standing here now, trimmed down without even trying, in front of Rose and Barry's mirror, is because I've lost Lynda. 'Hardly worth it for a few fucking abs,' I mutter bitterly. Not in a million fucking years. It's odd how so many things that you once thought were important turn out to be of no real importance whatsoever. Like I say: be careful what you wish for. For the first time in my life, I properly understand what that means.

If I'm completely honest, though, I am surprised I've lost quite so much weight considering the red wine – and white, come to think of it – that I've been knocking back without Lynda around. Although we could both be as bad as each other when it came to 'just another glass . . .' we were pretty good at keeping each other on the wagon as well. Once we'd both jumped on it, that is . . .

I honestly don't know how I'd have reacted had Lynda carried on drinking like she'd been doing before Jean's accident. Fortunately I didn't have to make that decision.

The morning after the accident, when she woke up and realized I'd gone I was already back in Spain. Lynda was deeply ashamed of herself for not being there when her sister had needed her.

I was still furious with her, I spent the whole of that day and night fielding phone calls and messages from her. She was crying her eyes out and saying how sorry she was and begging me to forgive her and give her another chance. But

I wanted to give her time to realize just how angry I was about it.

When I finally answered her at 6.30 a.m. on my way to the bank on Tuesday morning, it must have been her fiftieth attempt. She promised, between sobs, that she'd stop drinking. 'That's not what I want you to do Lynda,' I explained. 'I just want you to cut it back when I am around.'

I'd been praying she would see sense and she had. She stopped there and then. To her credit, that's what happened, and we entered our new dry phase. Was it a happier time? Yes I suppose it was. And much healthier, of course.

Together, it wasn't even difficult to do. It was at this point that Lynda's career was really starting to take off, after appearing as a guest on *Loose Women*, then becoming a regular panellist.

I'd already asked Lynda to marry me a couple of times and she'd turned me down, saying she was too old. I was disappointed at the time. I can understand where she was coming from now. I'm heading for sixty, which was the age she was when we finally tied the knot.

I am not so naive as to believe that I won't ever end up with another woman, as Lynda wanted me to do. But I do know that I will never marry again. Never. Not at my age.

What would be the point? I've just had the best marriage anyone could wish for.

Age wasn't the only reason Lynda didn't want to rush into marriage. While we both knew that our feelings for each other were genuine, she was concerned that, emotionally, she was a bit wobbly to say the least. She'd lost both her adoptive parents within such a short space of each other and had been devastated. She wanted to be sure that wasn't why she'd clung to me. She was also conscious of the mistakes she'd made in choosing her previous husbands and she wanted to be 100 per cent certain that she was doing the right thing hitching up with me.

I am a very patient man anyway so I was prepared to wait and give her as much time as she wanted. I didn't pressurize her at all, even though putting a ring on her finger was what I wanted more than anything in the world.

It didn't take long though before Lynda realized it was what she wanted as well. It happened in the solicitor's office of all places. He'd pointed out that the tax benefits would be so much better if we were married, and she could no longer see any reason to say no.

'OK, let's get married then!' she said, looking me straight in the eye and grinning like a Cheshire cat. Typical Lynda! Always one for a surprise in the most unlikely place. We both burst out laughing at the solicitor's shocked face as we tried to explain that we were very much in love as well and we'd already talked about it. We weren't doing it to stop the taxman getting his hands on too much of our hard-earned wedge.

The next time I asked her was when we were having dinner at The Ivy, a regular celeb haunt and one of ours because we loved the food there. Lynda always had the foie gras or steak tartare.

Ever the old romantic, I wanted to do the job properly (far away from the solicitor's office!), so I had gone out and bought her a whopping diamond engagement ring. It cost me a small fortune, but I figured she was worth it! Every last carat.

When Lynda went to the ladies, I gave the waiter the nod and ordered two glasses of champagne, asking him to pop the ring into Lynda's. It worked a treat – when they arrived, Lynda looked at me in amazement because we weren't drinking.

'Go on, just this once,' I coaxed.

She took a sip of her champagne and realized straight away there was something strange about it; a weird metallic taste for a start. Fumbling around, she fished out the ring and I slipped it on her finger as tears welled up in our eyes. We always were a soft-hearted pair!

As I said, I am never one to do things by halves and I was determined that her third wedding would be her last. And best. It was the same with her funeral. I wanted to make sure that Lynda got what she deserved on both occasions. The works.

We'd planned to get married at Christmas because not only was it Lynda's favourite time of year but we didn't want to wait too long. But another bombshell was just around the corner. Her sister Barbara was diagnosed with lung cancer in February 2007 and we had to postpone our plans.

Once again, Lynda was devastated. 'More than anything I hated the fact that I couldn't make her better,' she'd say for years after Barbara died, aged just fifty-six, in October 2007. Boy, do I know that feeling now, my lover.

I was completely out of my depth when it came to dealing with cancer. While I may no longer be frightened of dying, I have to admit that I am frightened of getting cancer. It is such a fucking cruel disease. What it does to the whole family is scary. Lynda used to say that I was bigger and braver than her because, although we shared the same hopes and dreams, I was the one who actually made them happen. She was too quick to accept that they were just dreams. But she was wrong. The way she faced cancer and her death with such dignity was incredible. Braver than I'll ever be.

Typical Lynda, though, once again she used her experience to try to help other people. Just as she had with Barnardo's, after Barbara's death she supported a national government campaign to raise awareness of lung cancer to urge people to see a doctor if they showed any signs. She did the same for Alzheimer's after seeing what her mum went through.

'If I can use my family's loss to save others, I will do all I can,' she used to say. Little did she realize then that she'd end up using her own death to achieve the same ends. What a star.

At her memorial, Maria McDonagh from the Alzheimer's Society, of which Lynda was an ambassador, recalled how she first met Lynda at a parliamentary lobby and discovered she was a 'fighter from day one'.

'She continued to be a voice for all those affected by dementia as her adoptive mother Ruth had dementia and she was to learn later in life that her birth mother was also diagnosed with the condition.

'Lynda always did her best to make sure their voices were heard – and loudly,' she added. 'We quickly learned nobody could say no when asked by Lynda Bellingham. No one dared!' she said, before making everyone laugh describing how she once opened a conference by waltzing across stage with the charity's chief executive officer.

'We tried to count up how many times Lynda Bellingham, ambassador extraordinaire, came to our aid and we simply lost count. Too many; too often.'

That was Lynda. To a tee.

When it came to fighting for herself, though, she was nowhere near as feisty. She'd stand her ground for any underdog, any worthy cause, or any friend or member of her family, until she was blue in the face. But she never had the same fire in her belly when it was anything very personal to herself. 'You can't keep taking shit all your life,' I'd tell her.

I'd like to think that the message did eventually sink in a little and that I did make her stand up for herself a bit more. If she didn't get a part, I urged her to call the casting director and ask why. Confront them. Over the money as well if need be. Lynda used to try to explain, in her own defence, that you could never put a price on loving what you do for a living and she would laugh at my talk about 'wedges' (a common building site phrase for wads of cash). On one of my birthdays she even asked Jean to make me a cake in the shape of a wedge as a surprise. We had a right laugh over it.

Some of my lessons in real-life work practices must have struck a chord when her agent told her that the *Calendar Girls* bosses had asked her to audition for the part of Annie in the play, instead of the lead role of Chris, as they'd agreed earlier. Lynda was in floods of tears. I told her to tell them where to get off and this time she actually took my advice on board and acted on it.

'In the words of Mr Spain, tell them to fuck off,' she said to her agent and put the phone down.

All her hours of preparation had been to read for the Chris role and it was the one part that she really, really wanted. For once, she'd stood her ground and said no, she wanted to read for Chris, not Annie. She bloody got it as well. The rest is almost showbiz history.

It was an important lesson for her and, bit by bit, I do believe she began to value her own worth more all round, with me there beside her. It was strange to me. She had this deep, unshakeable faith in her own ability as an actress, and rightly so. Judging by reaction to the news that Lynda was dying, the public agreed. One hundred per cent. Everybody and their mothers loved Lynda. Yet that didn't stop her getting horribly nervous every single time she went on stage.

Even when she'd been treading the boards for years in *Calendar Girls*, she was still absolutely terrified by the thought of delivering her character's Big Speech – the rousing one to the Women's Institute bigwigs – at the Royal Albert Hall in October 2012.

All her past triumphs counted for nothing. It was like the first time all over again, and of course she was bloody brilliant. She went down a storm. Job done, Lynda. Once again.

It was an emotional occasion organized to celebrate the end of the original real life *Calendar Girls*' fundraising after thirteen years. The good ladies of Rylstone WI would be keeping their clothes on from now on, after having raised over £3 million for Leukaemia & Lymphoma Research by taking them off. Lynda admired them greatly and desperately wanted the gala night to be a huge hit for them.

Little did either of us realize that, as she was getting nervous about the event, her cancer wasn't just lurking round the corner – it was already at work. Nine months or so down the line and Lynda would know for sure. She'd officially be a cancer patient herself, facing chemotherapy and colostomy bags and all the rest of it. Bless her heart.

And before too long, I'd find myself without her and trying to raise money myself for charities to research this vile disease in Lynda's name. If only we'd known what was to come, B? Could we have done anything about it? Anything at all? Probably not, I know, but it doesn't stop me asking the question. Over and over again. It haunts me to this day. And it is the one question I will never know the answer to. If only. Fucking if onlys . . .

Coming across so many actors during my time with Lynda, I realized that they're all the same when it comes to suffering stage fright before putting themselves out there. Running on nervous energy the lot of them are when they're on stage. Lynda always reckoned that it was the butterflies that kept them all on their toes. When the cast came off stage they'd be on a high, until they came back down to earth to worry about what the critics were going to say the next day. What a stressful job! You've really got to want to do it. And there was never any doubt in her mind or mine that Lynda did.

I had my first taste of 'performing' to the critics when it came to our wedding day on 31 May 2008, Lynda's sixtieth birthday.

Third time lucky for her, she always used to say. It was only the second time for me. I was the lucky one, though. I've always felt that I had a guardian angel looking after me. My life hasn't always run smoothly, but it's been fun and varied. Rich in experience! If only that luck hadn't run out when it did.

Apart from the births of Michael and Robbie, Lynda used to say our wedding was the happiest day of her life. I was determined that the new Mrs Bellingham Pattemore would have a day to remember, followed by a wonderful wedding night in 'our place', the Athenaeum. And she did; we both did. It took some serious planning and a fair bit of dosh, though that pressure was eased by a deal Lynda had struck up with *Hello!* magazine to cover the event.

The last thing she wanted was for her wedding to turn into a media circus (thankfully it didn't), but she had a lot of friends she needed to invite if she was going to do it properly. Lynda had an image to keep up and that was all going to cost. I've already told you what the champagne bill was! Thirty grand! And we didn't even get a bubble of it – unless you count the sparkling water.

This was one day we didn't need alcohol, though. Sorry for sounding so corny but we were high enough on pure emotion. We truly loved each other and the prospect of married life together was blissful. We had so many plans ... That feeling never wore off until Lynda was diagnosed. And even then, we remained happy, confident and positive we could beat it. For a good while.

Although not all of Lynda's friends had welcomed me with open arms, there was one guy I'd hit it off with straight away and that was Peter Delaney. The Archdeacon Peter Delaney, no less.

He accepted me the first day he met me and I've come to love him to bits. Lynda had known him, through Christopher Biggins initially, for thirty-odd years and had huge respect for him. I could see why, especially after we got off to a slightly embarrassing start.

Biggins was in panto at the time in Nottingham with the ex-*Brookside* actress Claire Sweeney. I'm assuming it was probably Christmas time 2005. Me and Lynda had gone to watch, as had Peter, and we were all going out for a meal together afterwards. I'd never met Claire before either but she seemed a really lovely lady and I remembered that she'd done some adverts for a company I used to work for in

Spain. I brought the subject up and it turned out that we knew some of the same people. All of a sudden she started laughing. She remembered hearing a funny story about a guy getting caught with his pants down out there. (I won't repeat it here and, in my defence, it was when I was foot-loose and fancy free after my marriage break up. Way before I met Lynda or the previous lady in my life, I hasten to add.)

Anyway, Claire put two and two together and wanted to know if that had been me. I confessed, a little bit sheep-ishly, that it was. I'd already told Lynda everything about what happened so it wasn't a shock to her. But I was embar-rassed for the story to be repeated in front of a man of the cloth I'd only just met. I needn't have worried, though. Peter didn't even flinch or judge me one bit.

I soon gained a lot of respect for him; he's just such a genuinely nice guy. He had blessed Lynda's wedding to Nunzio (at a different church) but she'd had no worries that it might be bad luck for him to conduct our wedding as well. To be honest, I don't think either of us wanted any-body else to marry us. Peter – or should I give him his proper title and call him The Venerable Peter Delaney MBE – was absolutely perfect for the job.

And his beautiful church, St Stephen Walbrook, next door to the Mansion House in the City of London, was as well. After being destroyed by the Great Fire of London in

1666, it was designed by Sir Christopher Wren and built of thick, pale stone. It has a huge domed ceiling and a circular altar sculpted by Henry Moore. Lynda loved it there and went on Sundays whenever she could. Christmas Eve midnight Mass was her favourite service. Mine too. We went every year unless Lynda was in panto and couldn't get back home. She always liked to light candles for her parents.

After going to see Peter and explaining why it was important for us to get married there with him doing the ceremony, he said that with permission from the Bishop of London it would be possible. And there'd be no need for a civil ceremony beforehand. Phenomenal.

Thrilled by the news, we threw ourselves into organizing the Big Day. Lynda had never actually been married in church before but I had. My first wedding, to Janice, had been a big white affair at St Bartholomew's in Crewkerne. Yes, it was the same church where we'd held Lynda's funeral and where I was returning for Coral's. Boy, does that place hold some memories of my life.

We chose the Coq d'Argent rooftop restaurant across the road from the church for the wedding reception, and Lynda was thrilled because the owners had got permission for us to have fireworks. She loved fireworks, which was why I surprised everyone with them at her burial.

The idea was to have a big party to celebrate her sixtieth birthday as well as our wedding, and as a jokey surprise I bought her a Zimmer frame with a personalized number plate on it. Jean had made a little model of Lynda with the Zimmer on top of a cake shaped like a bus pass. It stood in the corner of the living room for ages afterwards and was quite a conversation piece!

No expense spared, we also had a wedding cake made by a local bakery. As I've said, Lynda had a very sweet tooth.

One thing she didn't want was to look like mutton dressed as lamb in a proper wedding dress. I told her not to worry, but nevertheless she started off planning a dress similar to an evening dress she already had. The snooty designer she first hired wasn't much help and in the end she thought to hell with it. On our way to the airport to fly off to the Gambia to rest and get a tan for our wedding photographs, we stopped off at a bridal shop on New Bond Street and Lynda found exactly what she wanted. Her bouquet had already been ordered to match the delicate white and pale pink peonies and sweet peas she wanted to fill the church with – including a bower where the photographs could be taken. Flowers and fireworks: two of Lynda's greatest loves! Once they were sorted, I knew that nothing could go wrong.

Standing nervously in my white tux next to Brad, who I'd asked to be my best man, I was waiting at the altar when

Lynda arrived. With a tear in my eye, I turned to watch her walk down the aisle. She looked amazing in that beautiful church, all in white lace, with Biggins and Nickolas Grace at her side, doing what her late father Don wasn't here to do and give her away. Two old friends who were back there with me, at Lynda's memorial service.

I like to think that I am friends with both of them now. I don't see them regularly but we've talked. I don't want to be a burden to anybody. Maybe burden is the wrong word. I am just trying to get on with my own life. As best as I can in the circumstances.

Lynda told me afterwards that all day she kept thinking about her mum, dad and Barbara, and how much she'd have loved them to be there on that special occasion.

'Death is such a big deal in these important Life moments,' she later wrote in *Lost and Found.* Oh, B, you are so, so right. Not just in the big moments though. The little, everyday ones are bloody hard without the woman you love by your side as well. God bless you.

Throughout the ceremony, I was so nervous that my hands were shaking, especially when it came to making our vows. Peter did us proud and it was a very moving service with beautiful hymns like 'Love Divine, All Loves Excelling'. Little did I imagine that the next time I'd hear all Lynda's friends and family singing together again would be at her funeral. And so soon after our wonderful day.

Six-and-a-half years. All of them phenomenal, just far, far too short, B.

After all the photos, it was party time. A double celebration with many of the famous milling around. Far too many to mention by name.

Those who hadn't been able to make the service or reception, like Christopher Timothy and Robert Lindsay, who both travelled down to Crewkerne to pay their last respects at her funeral, were part of a video I'd had put together where all Lynda's absent friends paid tribute to her on camera. She was so touched by that. The thing about Lynda was that she was so used to doing everything for everybody else, she was always overwhelmed when people did something kind for her. She was completely and utterly selfless.

If I had been shaking at the altar, I was even more nervous when it came to making my wedding speech. I now knew exactly what Lynda meant when she talked about always getting butterflies before she went on stage. I'd spent the holiday in the Gambia working out what to say and, in a room full of well-spoken, professional actors and actresses, I knew that I'd have my work cut out to pull it off.

As ever, I'd decided that honesty was the best policy. Lynda said a lot of the 300 or so people there wouldn't have known about my past, but I think that was probably a bit naive. Or else she was just protecting my feelings. I'd made bloody headlines in the national press for being wanted by the FBI! How many people did she know who could say the same thing had happened to them?

Of course she was ready for anybody who dared to criticize me. As she told the press afterwards: 'He was a small pawn in a financial scam. Michael has done his stint and it should be left to rest. Ours is a relationship between two people who love and respect one another. These are all the things I've ever expected from a relationship but never had. To be honest, I still can't quite believe it.'

She always had a way with words, my wife! A friend of a friend who didn't know her but saw her on TV discussing the ins and outs of some worthy cause just before she was ill remarked afterwards, 'She spoke more eloquently than any politician I've ever heard!' Hear, hear. Lynda for Prime Minister! She'd have been bloody brilliant.

She didn't need to speak out to defend me, though. As long as my past didn't threaten to affect Lynda's career and reputation, I didn't really care what people thought of me personally. Take me or leave me. I have no time for snobbery or judgement without knowing me or the full facts.

Besides, I wasn't hiding anything. I'd already made up my mind to come straight out with it; confess and tell the truth about my past in my speech. The truth, the whole truth and nothing but the truth. Yes, I'd made mistakes in my life and I'd paid for them. A bit unconventional for a wedding speech, I know, but it was important to clear the air.

It wasn't all about me, though! I did remember to mention my wonderful new wife in all of this.

'I want to be serious now,' I told them. 'I want to reassure those of you who love Lynda – and that's not just the entire room but most of the country – that she is safe with me.

'She's had many frightening years without someone at her side. Well I'm not frightened. I won't run away. And I am on her side.

'I may not look like a knight but she is my lady and I will be strong for her. She's had to be strong on her own for far too long. Now she can lean on me. With the help of Michael and Robbie and all of you, I will make it my life's work to make her life happy and secure.'

As I sat down afterwards, I was amazed when everybody started clapping. Looking round I could see many of them had tears in their eyes as well. Yet I'd only spoken what was truly in my heart. And I had meant every single, last word of it.

If only I'd known how soon those words would be put to the test. Or how helpless I would feel when I could no longer keep my promise to always protect her.

I tried my best; I really fucking tried. But the cancer was just too big for both of us in the end. All I can console myself with now is that Lynda knew how much I tried. She knew how much I loved her and how I would have done anything I could to save her. I just hope to God that somewhere, up there, she still does.

CHAPTER 6

REMEMBER PRESTON?

......

For the time of year, it's a glorious, warm, sunny day, and here I am sitting in a hotel restaurant in Preston of all places.

Looking out of the window, I notice all the hundreds, if not thousands, of bluebells under the old oak trees across the rough, wide lawns. Beautiful, but they probably won't last too much longer.

Lynda loved seeing the spring flowers come out. Her real favourites were violets because they reminded her of her late adoptive mum Ruth. It's the first year she'll have missed them and yet they're dying already. It's a painful sign of how quickly time is marching on without her. Another season been and gone, and I'm already closer to the first anniversary of Lynda's death than I am to the day of her death itself. Weird. Especially as I don't feel I've really moved on anywhere myself in half a year.

I'm up here in Preston the middle of May for a business lunch. I haven't picked the hotel myself, but I easily could have done. It's not all grim Up North as we southerners are sometimes led to believe.

I don't think me and Lynda ever came to Preston with *Calendar Girls* but I could be wrong. After several long tours together, the towns and cities all sort of mingled into one. I can remember us being in Blackpool because a plaque was erected in tribute to Lynda near the theatre there before she died. She also did a fundraising Memory Walk for the Alzheimer's Society in Blackpool with children from a local primary school.

This is the sort of old country house hotel we might have stayed in. Lynda would have liked it and all I can think as I look at the menu is: *What would Lynda have chosen?* Probably not the lamb like me, which tastes good but not as good as her Sunday roast. How could it?

I can't be in Preston, of course, without hearing Lynda's naughty voice in my ear coming out with that saucy line everybody knows from the Oxo adverts. At Lynda's memorial in February, Jan Etherington, who cast Lynda as the middle-aged divorcee Faith Grayshott in the comedy *Second Thoughts*, and its sequel, *Faith in the Future*, said she'd never seen in another actress that 'complete mix of vamp and earth mother' that Lynda had shown when she leaned across the table and said to her Oxo husband: 'And, Michael . . . Remember Preston?'

My eyes automatically wander from the bluebells to the inner restaurant door leading to the big old staircase going upstairs. Even though I'm not staying here, I start to wonder what the bedrooms are like. And I wish, more than anything in the world, that I was sharing a bed in one of them with my Lynda tonight.

On the way to the railway station later that day, to catch my six o'clock train back to London, the friendly Indian taxi driver wants to know what brings me to Preston. It's his hometown and a place he's obviously very proud of. I tell him it's just business, and we have a bit of banter about the north versus the south and which is best. I tell him that nowhere beats Somerset and he tells me which famous people have come from Preston, including the *Wallace and Gromit* creator Nick Park, and some big oil company boss I've never heard of.

As we get talking, he gets on to his family, of which he's just as proud, and reveals how his last wife left him for his best mate. I don't usually need much of a cue to talk about Lynda and so, of course, I find myself telling him about my own loss.

'Have you heard of the actress Lynda Bellingham?' I ask him.

'Oh yeah! She was a really lovely lady, wasn't she?' he replies. 'And didn't she mention Preston in one of them Oxo adverts?'

She was and she did, I tell him, before we pull up at the entrance to the railway station, where I jump out quickly to catch the London train home, feeling even more alone than when I'd arrived that morning.

Part Two

CHAPTER 7

GLASS HALF FULL AGAIN

......

It's late on 31 December 2012, and I'm pouring two glasses of nicely chilled pink champagne for me and Lynda. It's our favourite tipple and we've decided that we can now safely handle the odd glass or two without too much trouble. Amazing what you can still learn about yourselves at fifty-seven and sixty-four (then find out you were wrong all over again when things go pear-shaped).

After years of being on the wagon, we'd fallen off and broken our strict booze ban on a recent holiday in Tenerife. I'd looked across at another couple enjoying a bottle of cold white wine together in the hot sunshine and seen the condensation running down the glass.

Turning to Lynda, I'd asked her, 'Do you think we'll

ever be able to have just one glass of wine?' 'No, not really,' she'd replied. But we decided to give it a go anyway.

And so far, so good. Well, apart from a trashy women's magazine picking up on the story and running it on the front cover with an old, unflattering picture of Lynda walking out onto the street through a stage door with no make-up on, under the headline: 'Lynda: Back on the booze!'

Apart from that, it was all good. We hadn't been going mad, drinking a glass or two, and it had actually made our social lives a bit easier. People at parties no longer quizzed us non-stop about why we were teetotal and then felt the need to explain how 'little' they drank themselves.

We are in a hotel room in Bradford where Lynda is appearing in panto at the nearby Alhambra Theatre. Panto is a tiring job; one of the most exhausting jobs an actor can do, she says.

The audience come to see the stars of the show – in this case Lynda and Billy Pearce – and they demand 100 per cent. Most of them are children who don't sit still, and it requires a lot of energy to entertain them. Lynda jokes that as the run goes on her fairy godmother character has developed into a cross between a nice granny and a grumpy headmistress. Only she sees that; I never notice and I'm sure the kids and their parents don't either. She is a total pro at all times.

Lynda gets on very well with Billy, who is playing Buttons, and he's been kind enough to invite us to a lovely party at his home on the outskirts of the city. We had a good time, then left to head back to our bedroom at Bradford's Great Victoria Hotel.

Lynda was never a big believer in New Year's Eve. At least not since I'd met her. She'd always thought it a bit naive that people could think life could magically change for the better on the stroke of midnight. She always thought it was the wrong time of year to be making resolutions that you probably had little chance of sticking to in miserable January. Of course, what hadn't registered with her that night – or me for that matter – was that life could actually get a lot worse on the stroke of midnight. Not straight away but soon enough, soon enough ...

Back then, the future was looking bright. We had lots of plans for 2013, including a family celebration for Lynda's sixty-fifth birthday at the end of May. We'd looked into taking everyone to Florida but the cost of flying out a party of seven adults and three kids had put us off and we were now planning to book Center Parcs at Longleat in Wiltshire instead.

By the beginning of February, Lynda had finished panto and we were heading back home to London and looking forward to climbing into our own bed for the first time in two months.

The boys, Lynda's and mine, definitely hadn't inherited either of our genes for tidiness, because we arrived home to find a dishwasher full of dirty plates and a kitchen floor knee deep in crumbs. Like me, Lynda cannot work in a mess and she immediately set about cleaning up so the decks were clear for her to settle down and plan the final edit for her first novel, *Tell Me Tomorrow*. Most of the book had been written in hotel rooms and dressing rooms on tour between performances of *Calendar Girls* and panto. She never gave herself a minute off.

I'd love to tell her that nothing has changed on the domestic front since she left us. I doubt she'd be surprised. Lynda insisted on leaving everywhere sparkling clean, even joking that she was dusting in circles. But she wasn't daft enough to believe that it would stay like that for long when she was no longer with us. Boys really don't listen to anything about cleaning and tidying, I've discovered. Only this morning, I found that Brad and Robbie had stripped their beds and put the sheets in the wash, when I'd specifically told them not to do so because the cleaners wouldn't be coming in this Wednesday as they normally do. Well they'll just have to dry the sheets and iron them themselves! The only time

I've ironed anything for them was on the day of Lynda's funeral, when I did all their shirts to make sure they were absolutely pristine for their mum. Unlike Lynda, I refuse point blank to clean up after them. If I had a pound for every time I'd told them 'I'm not your mother!' when faced with their mess, I'd be a bloody billionaire.

It was only a couple of months earlier that we'd been to hospital in Bradford on Christmas Eve, and Lynda had started popping the indigestion tablets which eased things a bit for her. But – Sod's Law – if she didn't come down with a nasty chest infection that had started on the day of her last panto performance.

Her first night under our own duvet and Lynda couldn't sleep a wink for coughing and wheezing. I'd never had a problem sleeping in my life, but even I was kept awake. More practice for what lay ahead, I suppose now.

I picked her up from her private doctor's practice on Harley Street the next day. She'd been given a prescription for antibiotics. Not the most patient of patients at that point, she was so anxious to speed up her recovery that her first few days off were spent with her head over a bowl of hot Karvol steam and guzzling cough medicine and throat pastilles. At the same time, she had a stool test done which came back negative, all clear.

As soon as the chest infection cleared up, we set about enjoying ourselves a bit more in some of her free time. Believe it or not, one of our first outings was straight back up north to watch *The Full Monty* stage play at the Lyceum Theatre in Sheffield. We both enjoyed it as much as the film and, for once, Lynda was glad to be in the audience not the cast.

Michael and Robbie both had big birthdays that year as well. Michael was turning thirty and Robbie twenty-five, so as a special present, Lynda had paid for them to go to Los Angeles together in February. It was a working trip for Michael, who was there for the film industry's pilot season to suss out any acting opportunities and meet a few people. In the hotel business himself, Robbie was there to support his brother and pick up a few tips about American hotels, as well as to soak up the sunshine. Lynda had always dreamt of cracking Hollywood herself and she had high hopes that Michael might strike lucky one day. She was also very proud of Robbie for working so hard and doing so well in his junior management job at the Athenaeum. Those hotel walls could tell him a tale or two! Aside from that, though, she wanted Michael and Robbie to enjoy each other's company and make the most of some brother bonding. Family was never far from the front of her mind.

'I'm so thrilled they're doing this,' she kept saying. 'All

parents want their children to get on well together, so they have each other when they're no longer around. I'm no different.'

I know what she meant. I'm just the same with Stacey and Brad. I suppose family is not something that either of us takes for granted. Looking back it is quite uncanny some of the things that Lynda used to say without realizing what was to come.

We had our own plans, or should I say, The Plan, to travel as well. We were going to work really hard and save up as much money as we could for the next five years and then slow down a bit. We wanted to move to my old stomping ground in the West Country that I love so much. Ideally we wanted to buy a property that we could do up to our own taste. Lynda, who always hoped she'd just keel over and die on stage at a grand old age, was to keep a flat in London for when she was working in town. It didn't work out quite like that, though, did it, Babes?

Around that time, I remember the two of us talking about the past as well as the future, and what we'd have done differently. I think it stemmed from some Irish newspaper asking Lynda what she'd write today in a letter to her younger self.

I'm not sure whether she did the letter in the end but she certainly thought about it carefully before telling me, 'I think I'd have to tell myself to take things more slowly.

Decisions can wait, and sometimes it's better to do nothing than do something wrong,'

We had no idea, of course, of the decisions we were going to have to face soon enough. And these were ones that couldn't wait. Without us knowing it, time was the one thing Lynda no longer had much of. She always took her deadlines very seriously, whether it involved her writing or acting. And here she was facing the biggest deadline of her life without knowing it. It wasn't even in her bloody diary.

Valentine's Day was in her diary, though. Like Mother's Day, it was always a bit too commercial for Lynda's liking. She didn't like forced emotion unless, of course, it was for an acting role, and she preferred things to be a bit more spontaneous. But she knew I liked giving and receiving cards on every occasion. I'm a bit of an old softie like that! She didn't forget and we both had a lovely evening that year back at St Stephen Walbrook, where Peter Delaney was hosting a fundraising dinner.

The whole church was lit by candles and it looked absolutely beautiful. Tables had been set up inside, where three-course dinners would be served. The lady in charge of catering there did such a fantastic job that night. Little did I ever think that I'd be hiring her before too long to make canapés to hand round after Lynda's memorial . . .

The musical actors Marti Webb and Gay Soper both

sang after dinner and Lynda did a reading. We had a fantastic time reliving the memories of our wedding day in that same church almost five years earlier.

'Now that's what I do call romantic,' Lynda told me on the way home. Happy days. And nights.

Before too long, it was back to work and we were on the road again, with Lynda filming the ITV Sunday morning series *Country House Sunday*, for most of March and April. Lynda was in her element when the call had come through asking her to do what she described as 'a sort of *Downton* for daytime!' It came on the back of her success in *My Tasty Travels*, which she'd done the year before.

The series involved a tour of the country's stately homes and she was really looking forward to it. It also filled in a handy work gap for her until she headed for Sheffield for the start of the stage play *A Passionate Woman*.

The play only had a very small cast and Lynda was to play the part of Betty, based on writer Kay Mellor's true story about her mother. For thirty years Kay's mother had kept it a secret that she'd had a love affair with a neighbour. He had been killed by his jealous wife after she learnt he was about to leave her for Kay's mother. It was when they were doing the washing up one day that Kay's mother finally broke down and confessed her heartache to her daughter.

It was a juicy part playing Betty that Lynda couldn't

wait to get her teeth into, and she was also looking forward to being Christopher Timothy's 'wife' again. All these other husbands; I had such a lot of competition! Thankfully it was always me she came back to. And, without sounding too cocky or arrogant, I always knew she would. Jealousy was never a problem for either of us. We trusted each other completely.

The play was set to run until the following March and, once again, I was to be back working on my laptop. I sometimes think I did as many miles on the road with Lynda as I'd been doing when I commuted to and from Spain for all those years. Not that I am complaining about touring with Lynda. Far from it. I'd give anything to be doing it all over again and fighting off jelly caterpillars in the car!

No sooner had Lynda finished *Country House Sunday*, when she received another invitation, but this time it was one that made her heart sink. It was from a Harley Street clinic for free liposuction, and she was convinced it had been sent because they'd watched her on television and thought she needed it. I tried to tell her she was putting two and two together and making five, but it didn't do her ego much good. Although she always admitted that her body confidence was low, Lynda had never been tempted to have any cosmetic surgery. As far as she was concerned, it was a slippery slope. Once you start, where do you draw the line? True, she had had her nose fixed years earlier but

It looks like I am thinking 'where the hell is she?' But actually it was just a fun pose for the camera. I knew Lynda wouldn't be late because she never was and I was right. She arrived bang on time at 4pm for our wedding on 31 May 2008.

We do! Making our wedding vows in front of our good friend The Venerable Peter Delaney MBE at the beautiful St Stephen Walbrook church in the city of London. Almost seven years later, it is where Lynda's memorial service was held.

This picture is a very special one to me because my dad Joe is in the background on the right of Nickolas Grace, as we sign the register. Like Lynda, he is sadly no longer with us. I like the picture because I know how much he thoroughly enjoyed our wedding day.

Lynda's sixtieth birthday cake complete with a little model of her on a Zimmer frame and a new bus pass in reference to her age! It was made by her sister Jean and presented to Lynda at our wedding reception. She loved it.

During my wedding speech, I presented Lynda with her wedding present from me – a real Zimmer frame complete with her own personalised number plate! She laughed like hell when one of the staff at the reception at the Coq d'Argent wheeled it in.

OXO MUM FALLS FOR £1/2M CON JAILBIRD

TV Lynda's saucy dates

I know it's early days but I love him, says Lynda Bellingham

Is Oxo mum's affair with fraudster another recipe for disaster?

Hitting tabloid newspaper headlines for all the wrong reasons.
Me and Lynda a recipe for disaster? I don't think so!

Mr and Mrs on holiday at Peter Island in the British Virgin Islands the year after our wedding in November 2009. Lynda was writing a travel piece for a national newspaper and this picture was taken on the balcony of our hotel suite. Happy days.

Celebrating our fourth anniversary in Malaysia, 31 May 2012. Lynda was working hard on her novel *Tell Me Tomorrow* when we were over there but I am glad to say she took time off to mark the occasion. The hotel staff presented us with this little chocolate gesture at the end of our special dinner.

The wonderful staff surprised us a second time by scattering rose petals on our bed in the shape of a heart and a figure '4' to commemorate the years. It was a lovely touch.

The two most important women in my life: Lynda with my daughter Stacey in the kitchen of our lodge at Center Parcs, Longleat, where the whole family celebrated Lynda's sixty-fifth birthday and our fifth wedding anniversary in May 2013.

My collapsed fifth anniversary cake! Lynda ordered it as a surprise and sneaked it into the car boot when we travelled to Center Parcs but hadn't banked on it melting in the heat. It may look disgusting but it still tasted bloody good!

Lynda with the grandchildren – Stacey's boys Cooper and Oakley and Michael's son Sacha (middle) at Center Parcs.

A sixty-fifth birthday hug for their old mum from Michael and Robbie at Center Parcs, May 2013.

On the red carpet arriving at the Olivier Awards ceremony in May 2013, where Lynda was to present the best actor in a musical award with Queen's Brian May. This was taken before we knew about her cancer.

Lynda outside Buckingham Palace after receiving her OBE in March 2014. A proud day for us all.

Precious, precious memories of our very last holiday together in Corfu in September 2014, just weeks before I lost her.

I love this picture so much I had it blown up to poster size and put up in church for her memorial service. It is now hanging on my lounge wall. It was taken during a magazine shoot before she was ill and, to me, that is Lynda: sexy, sassy and one incredibly attractive lady.

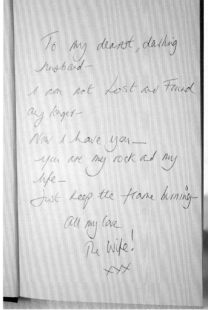

To my dearest, darling husband –
I am not Lost and Found any longer –
Now I have you –
you are my rock and my life –
Just keep the frame burning –
all my love
The Wife!
XXX

I was always in awe of Lynda's beautiful handwriting. What a lovely example I have here in the inscription to me in her first memoir, *Lost and Found*. The note was only added a month before she died so they truly are precious words.

Putting on a brave face after losing Lynda. This family photo was taken just before Christmas 2014 and is the shot I used for my personal Christmas card. I am pictured with Michael, Robbie, Bradley, Stacey and my grandsons Cooper and Oakley.

Lynda pictured with Star, Michael and Robbie's pet sheepdog who died before I met Lynda. This is the picture the medium Yvonne Williams referred to that is above the television in our bedroom. I have no idea when or where it was taken.

THE CURTAIN WENT UP
MAY 31ST 1948

THE FINAL CURTAIN CAME DOWN
19TH OCTOBER 2014

ACTRESS, AUTHOR
AND PRESENTER

A UNIQUE LOVING
MOTHER AND WIFE

10 YEARS WASN'T ENOUGH
HAPPY BIRTHDAY AND HAPPY
WEDDING ANNIVERSARY FROM
YOUR LOVING HUSBAND MICHAEL xxx

The cards that accompanied the special flowers on Lynda's grave on 31 May 2015. It would have been Lynda's sixty-seventh birthday and our seventh wedding anniversary. Our first apart.

GOD SAW THAT YOU WERE GETTING
TIRED, A CURE WAS NOT TO BE SO HE
PUT HIS ARMS AROUND YOU AND
WHISPERED "COME WITH ME" WITH
TEARFUL EYES I WATCHED YOU
FADE AWAY ALTHOUGH I
LOVED YOU DEARLY I
COULD NOT MAKE YOU
STAY A GOLDEN HEART
STOPPED BEATING HARD
WORKING HANDS TO REST
GOD BROKE OUR HEARTS TO
PROVE TO US HE ONLY TAKES THE BEST
LOVE MICHAEL XXX

A rose for my rose. The Royal Horticultural Society unveiled a specially grown rose named in memory of Lynda at Hampton Court in June, 2015. She would have been thrilled.

Here I am visiting the historic, very spiritual sanctuary of Machu Picchu in April 2015. It was an inspiring trip.

From one graveside to another . . . My very moving trip to the D-Day landing beaches and war graves in Normandy included a visit to the immaculately maintained American cemetery overlooking Omaha Beach. I am pictured there in June, 2015, after setting off on my journey on this special anniversary on 31 May 2015.

that had more to do with camera angles and boosting her chances of landing acting parts than just vanity. So, saying no to liposuction, she headed straight for the treadmill in our bedroom instead.

It was quite a busy time for her even though she was officially supposed to be 'resting'. Unlike in her younger days, of course, she no longer had to resort to cleaning jobs to pay the rent. I have no doubt whatsoever that, if she'd needed to, even at her late stage of life, Lynda would have just got on and done it. And she'd have found something positive to say about the experience. Nothing could beat my wife; well, almost nothing.

One of the fun things we'd been looking forward to was Helen Worth's wedding. We both liked Helen, who has a great sense of humour and, as Lynda always used to say, couldn't be more different to her downtrodden *Coronation Street* character, Gail, if she tried. We'd had dinner with Helen and her husband-to-be at the time they were house hunting; they needed two homes – one in the north and one in the south because of their jobs. People always think an actor's life is glamorous and it certainly has its moments, but a lot of the time it means a great deal of personal inconvenience, travelling and sheer hard work. You've got to really want to do it.

At the wedding reception at the Ritz, I'd been under strict instructions from Lynda not to call any of the guests by their soap character names. In her business it was an unforgivable sin, she said. Bloody hard thing to do when so many guests there were Helen's *Coronation Street* colleagues and it was a soap we watched. Fortunately I didn't slip up once, even if I did have to keep biting my tongue to stop myself saying the wrong thing.

Lynda was also thrilled and terrified at the same time when she was asked to attend the Olivier Theatre Awards at the Royal Opera House. She was thrilled because she considered it such an honour to be asked to present the award for Best Male Actor in a Musical to Michael Ball. But she was also terrified by the idea of having to step out of a car and onto the red carpet at such a big do. As old, talented and experienced as she was, she always dreaded those moments when she was on show in front of so many cameras.

It was only hearing a stranger's friendly voice in the crowd shouting 'Hello Lynda' that put her at ease when we arrived.

'Phew, somebody likes me!' was her grateful reaction. No good telling her that actually, Lynda, everybody likes you! Only then could she relax and sign autographs. She never minded doing that and didn't think much of other celebrities who moaned about it. 'Where would we be without fans?' she used to ask. Correct. Always had your feet firmly on the ground, didn't you, B?

She was also back on the panel of *Loose Women*, which she'd left very quietly the year before by choosing not to sign another contract. But this time it was only for a single episode as a guest. Jane McDonald caused a bit of a stir later at Lynda's funeral on this issue by saying Lynda hated doing *Loose Women*. What she was really getting at was that Lynda worried that the show made her look more like a television presenter rather than a serious actress. So when she bowed out, she did it discreetly, paving the way to go back if need be. She always felt very strongly that you should always leave doors open for yourself. Despite all her own acting success, she never forgot what a fickle business she was in. You could be top of the bill one day but nowhere to be seen the next. She never took anything for granted. Ever.

Unlike the rest of her family, who were all green fin-gered, Lynda was never a gardener. Not at all. She loved flowers more than most but just not the business of grow-ing them. She was thrilled, nonetheless, to be invited to Chelsea Flower Show that same month as an ambassador for the Alzheimer's Society.

She wasn't so thrilled when she arrived to join Ruth Langsford, Fiona Phillips, Arlene Phillips and Sally Lindsay for afternoon tea in the Memory Garden. In her high heels, she tripped over a little ledge and fell face first into a gravel path. Luckily her hands broke the fall, but she was very shaken by it and grateful to Ruth who came to her rescue.

It is easy to look back on every little incident that happened in that year and wonder if it was a sign that she wasn't well. And one I should have picked up on. What if? If only? Why didn't I do something ...? On this occasion, though, I don't think it was anything more sinister than a straightforward accident that could have happened to anybody. So I don't really need to beat myself up about it. But I still keep doing it; going over every minute detail with a fine toothcomb.

Thankfully, by now, we had got rid of one major stress that had been affecting us both for months and months. Now, I do really wonder what effect it all had on Lynda's poor health. Stress doesn't do anybody any favours.

It had been caused by a business rival of mine who had bad mouthed me, Lynda and my company Virtual Property World, of which Lynda was also a director, on the internet.

He'd written two vile, anonymous online blogs accusing Lynda of helping to run a company that might have been involved in property fraud, and accusing me of being a property fraudster. I've never been a property fraudster and there was nothing at all fraudulent about the company.

We guessed who was behind it straight away, and then had to prove it. It was no easy task and we risked losing a lot of money in legal bills and employing computer experts to carry out searches to trace the source and nail the culprit.

But because we felt so strongly about being lied about and bullied so publicly, we took the risk. It was an absolutely horrendous experience but it paid off when, out of court, businessman Darren Richards admitted he was accountable, apologized and was ordered to pay us a six figure sum in damages and costs.

Once she knew she was dying, Lynda always said she would haunt him. I hope she fucking is. Once again, my past had been twisted and used against me and Lynda at a traumatic time in our lives. Still, what goes around comes around. We both strongly believed that.

Mind you, I had to laugh when going through a drawer recently and finding the newspapers that carried the first story of Lynda going out with me. Was our relationship 'a recipe for disaster for the Oxo mum?' asked one of the headlines! I don't think so, do you, Babes? Those ten years were the best years of both our lives.

Soon enough, though, it was time to relax and celebrate Lynda's sixty-fifth birthday and our fifth wedding anniversary at Center Parcs. As much as she was looking forward to us all joining in the fun together, cycling and all the rest of it with our 'blended' family (isn't that what you call two families that come together?), Lynda had one strict rule for the trip.

Although she refused to be beaten by her age on most things, she was drawing the line at going on the water slides! And of course it would've been rude to abandon her so I didn't either ...

'While you're all getting soaked at high speed, I'll be taking sanctuary in the spa, treating myself to a facial,' she told the young ones.

But it was only after she'd 'earned' it – her words – by organizing the catering back at the chalet.

And, of course, being Lynda the food had to be fantastic. No easing up on standards even when she was on holiday. We had set off from London with the Range Rover boot absolutely heaving with food and drink. Too much, in fact, because we brought half of it back. Lynda had been determined that the family would party and, boy, we did.

While the young ones threw themselves into all the activities during the day, me and Lynda just chilled together. Most nights we'd cook steaks for everyone on the barbecue – or should I call it the bonfire? Stacey has since split up with her husband, Sam, who was the one responsible for lighting it! We all had such a laugh.

I wasn't complaining, though, as I wasn't called on to

make my signature barbecue dish of Guinness chicken, which is just how it sounds. A whole chicken with a full can of Guinness inside its arse! No fancy recipe but really tasty. To be done properly, it had to be cooked on a gas barbecue like the one we used at our villa in Spain. Well, that was my excuse ... I wish we'd never sold that place. We had some good times there. The patio was completely private and Lynda loved getting her kit off and sunbathing completely naked so she got an all-over tan. No white bits. She always went a fabulous colour really quickly, but we just weren't using the villa enough to warrant keeping it on. We'd sold her apartment first. (One year out in Moraira, Lynda had organized a surprise birthday party for me. Instead of flying out, we'd driven through France, stopping en route to visit friends in Bordeaux or Bergerac, I think. Of course Lynda used it as an excuse to empty the shelves of one French supermarket of all its foie gras. Naughty stuff but, boy, did she love it.)

Lynda didn't think it was so funny at Center Parcs, however, when she tried to surprise me with a special fifth wedding anniversary cake.

She'd ordered my favourite chocolate mousse cake from a local bakery. It's a Raymond Blanc recipe and the only dessert I'm really all that bothered about. Lynda had sneaked it into the boot behind my back. What she hadn't taken into account was the heat of the car and the long journey. Not surprisingly, when we arrived it had melted to a squidgy mush.

She hadn't opened the cake box and hadn't realized what had happened until we were all in a restaurant for the big family dinner on 31 May. Lynda's birthday. Don't ask me the logistics, but she had somehow got the cake delivered there earlier.

As soon as we arrived, I could see the waitress whispering to her and Lynda disappearing off into the kitchen. I wondered what was going on.

Nevertheless, the cake was served up. It may not have looked as good as it did when it left London, but I'm happy to say it tasted every bit as delicious as always. The thought was there and it gave us all another laugh.

As Lynda commented later in her column in *Yours* magazine: 'Only Mr Spain could have slight cause to disagree that my big birthday weekend at Center Parcs Longleat with our beloved family was anything less than perfect. But I know he wouldn't!'

Too right, Babes, I wouldn't! It was absolutely perfect. All the more perfect because it turned out to be our last family holiday together. Precious, precious memories now.

Looking back now, I realize Lynda was out of breath when we were riding the bikes you needed to get around at

Center Parcs. We'd hired three separate villas. Stacey and her family were in one; the boys were all bunked up in one and me and Lynda were in another. Ours was a bit further away and up a long hill.

Now Lynda was always a very fit woman – she had to be to go on stage with *Calendar Girls*. It was demanding work physically as well as mentally. She was also very competitive. If I was travelling at a thousand miles an hour, she'd have to go at a thousand and ten. She just wouldn't be beaten. The word wasn't even in her vocabulary. We used to have some right secret races up and down the hotel pools on play tours. She'd be lapping, I'd be lapping, then I'd speed up and she'd pretend not to notice. But as soon as I'd nearly levelled with her, she'd put a spurt on and beat me to the pool side and laugh. It was just how we were.

But suddenly – and apart from when I went flying into the ditch – she was lagging behind me, really struggling to keep up and out of breath. I kept on pedalling, thinking it was just a game as normal. But it wasn't normal. Not one bit.

It is only looking back that you see these things more clearly. As Lynda used to say throughout her illness, it is hard to see anything when you're in the eye of the storm. You have to wait for the dust to settle. Bang on right again, B. I realize that myself now.

It was the same when we went to Italy a few weeks later

in June. We were staying with our good friends Angie and John Chandler, at their villa in Tuscany. Don't get me wrong, we had a great time. We all spent hours sitting out in the sunshine playing Perudo, a dice game otherwise known as liar's dice. John and Angie introduced us to it and it had us all in hysterics. Lynda never forgave me for mistakenly thinking nine fours were thirty-two after a couple of glasses of vino! She, of course, had the upper hand because as an experienced actress she could bluff her way through the games better than any of us. It helped too, that she could also remember her times tables from her schooldays. Obviously I'd been relying on calculators for far too long.

As well as being great fun, Lynda kept pointing out that Perudo was good for the old memory. Remember she was an ambassador for the Alzheimer's Society! Thinking well ahead to Christmas, she was planning to buy several boxes to plant in some of her Christmas stockings. Christmas! If only we could have known how very different everything would be by Christmas . . .

One day out in Italy we'd been to a restaurant, then John had wanted to take us up a hill to another part of the old town, if I remember rightly. But Lynda, who'd been really breathless throughout the day, took one look at the hill we had to walk up and said, 'I can't do it.'

Hmmm. 'Can't' wasn't a word Lynda would use in

normal circumstances. Alarm bells were starting to ring. 'Hang on,' I thought. 'There's something major going on here. This isn't right.' Slipping out of earshot, I phoned Lynda's doctor in London, explained everything and asked, 'When we get back can I bring her in?'

Lynda didn't suspect anything; she was used to me being on the phone making work calls all the time we were away, anyway. Without telling her, I made the appointment for 10 a.m. the morning after we got back. The doctor had also arranged for her to have a scan.

By now, as I'd told the doctor, Lynda's stomach had swelled up like hell. It was a huge, hard bump under her summer dresses. Typical Lynda, she cracked jokes about having an alien in there but underneath the humour she was worried. I remember the two of us and Angie all furiously googling to find out what it could be, to come up with an answer, anything to reassure her: 'It could be this, B, or it could be that.' The last thing on my or anybody else's mind was cancer. Concerned as we all were, none of us guessed what was really going on. Or what lay ahead. Maybe it's just as well.

Returning home on the Wednesday, I told Lynda that I was taking her to see the doctor the next morning. To be honest, I think she was quite relieved.

Lynda was also plagued by a very painful frozen shoulder, and she was starting to wonder why it was that, when the body stops, it seems to fall apart?

As soon as her relentless work schedule had eased up a bit, the pain had struck. A chest infection, her stomach swelling and now a frozen shoulder. If you've ever had shoulder problems, you'll know how agonizing the pain can be.

Still, at least we had another holiday to look forward to: three whole weeks in Greece. Well, we called it a holiday, but Lynda was planning on working on her new novel over there, *The Boy I Love*. She'd written a lot of her first one *Tell Me Tomorrow* when we were on holiday in Malaysia and it had seemed to work well. She'd completed the rest of it while she was on tour.

I, of course, would be running my property development business, which I was now concentrating on, from my mobile phone and laptop. No rest for the wicked! Or us workaholics! While other people our age (except Lynda's showbiz pals who, like her, planned to tread the boards for as long as they could breathe) were thinking of slowing down and semi-retiring, both of us continued to be driven 100 per cent. We just had different motors driving us.

At least we knew that the hot sun on our backs would do us both good. Lynda was hoping it would ease her shoulder problems and she could stop guzzling painkillers every few hours. We were also planning to do as much work as we could in the first couple of weeks out there because John and Angie were flying out to join us for the last week of the holiday. More Perudo!

Unfortunately, we never made it as far as Gatwick airport, let alone hot, sunny Greece. Because we were about to discover that my beautiful, brave, kind, loving, sexy, funny wife and soulmate had cancer.

CHAPTER 8

THE LONGEST WALK
OF MY LIFE

......

Heads down and clinging to each other every step of the way, me and Lynda are stumbling down busy Harley Street in Central London together, trying to take in the devastating news we've just heard. It is Tuesday, 2 July 2013. A date, and a walk, never to be forgotten. Never, ever.

Twenty minutes earlier, we'd been sitting in front of the consultant surgeon, Mr Richard Cohen, who'd mistakenly thought we knew Lynda had cancer. All we'd been told by her usual doctor, a few days earlier, was that the scan had shown that she had a shadow on her liver. We must cancel our holiday to Greece and see this man.

'Cancer, what do you mean, cancer?' Lynda demanded to know, as we heard that dreaded word used for the first time.

We both stared at the doctor we'd only just met, but were soon going to get to know extremely well. He, in turn, stared at his computer screen, then straight back at Lynda before telling her, 'I am so terribly sorry. I thought you had already been informed of your position. You have cancer of the colon and lesions on your lungs and your liver.'

What?! I am ashamed to say that I started to sob and it was Lynda who was the first to comfort me. Not the other way round as, by rights, it should have been.

Putting her hand on my arm, she said, 'Don't cry, darling, it's going to be all right.' Only my wife could do that! Completely and utterly selfless even at a time like that. If she wasn't a saint then, she must be by now, surely. So many people have since been helped by the way she wrote and talked so openly about her struggle once she'd got her head round it and was ready to tell her story. Her way. It always had to be told her way.

'Can't you operate?' I managed to ask, after pulling myself together as much as I was physically able to do.

He explained that although his job as a sort of 'plumber' was to remove tumours, it was imperative that Lynda saw an oncologist and he'd made us an appointment with Professor Justin Stebbing. Another name we were going to come to know well.

In his opinion, Professor Stebbing was the best in the

business and his office was just down the road at the London Oncology Clinic.

So off we went, reeling from the shock, from number 116 to number 95 Harley Street. As I've told people ever since, it was the longest walk of my entire life. No ifs nor buts about it.

At the end of it, I was expecting us to be told by Professor Stebbing to go home and put our affairs in order because Lynda was going to die. Sooner rather than later.

Then we were sitting opposite another doctor who looked very young. More like a head boy, Lynda used to say, than a doctor we were going to come to rely on for her dear life.

But he had a nice manner and he tried to explain simply that he understood we were both in shock and that nothing right now was going to make sense to either of us. Correct, Professor.

'But it is important you understand that having cancer does not mean you are going to die, Lynda,' he said. And I've never been as grateful to hear anything in all my life. It lifted everything.

Even so, Lynda started going off on one about how she didn't want to be kept alive feeling like shit with no hair simply to prolong the agony for her and the family. And I was off again. Sobbing with my head in my heads. No bloody use to her at all.

Fortunately Professor Stebbing took control and told

her to stop the dramatic outburst, before he explained that cancer treatment had come a long way. This was what he planned to do ...

We listened as he went on to tell us how, from July to Christmas, she'd be blasted with a cocktail of strong chemotherapy drugs to try to shrink the main tumour in her colon and the secondaries in her liver and lungs. One of those chemo drugs is called fluorouracil, also known as FU2. It was an appropriate name and it was what Lynda christened her cancer. FU2 for Fuck U 2 !

One of things that we relied upon throughout all this was our black sense of humour. We'd both made living wills long before then and felt very strongly that we never wanted to be burdens to our family. Nor did we want to end our lives slowly with no quality of life either, whether it was from something like Alzheimer's or old age. Funnily enough, it had never crossed Lynda's mind that she'd get cancer. Nor mine. Strange really when it is so common and we'd both already seen our own family members die of it – for me it was my dad, and for Lynda, her sister Barbara. Lynda was also a long-time supporter of the Macmillan Cancer Support charity. So we were no fools and yet here we were in this position.

During our many conversations over the years about the end of life, the assisted suicide clinic Dignitas in

Switzerland had been mentioned as one option. But also, in dark humour mode, I'd promised Lynda that, should the time come, I'd hand her a bottle of brandy, put a fag in her mouth and push her off a cliff in her wheelchair. Of course I didn't really mean it; it is just the sort of daft thing you can say when you're not faced with a real dilemma.

Having said that, I have come to learn pretty much first-hand what the expression 'quality of life' really means. And just how important it is.

But back there and then in Justin's office, we weren't thinking along those lines. We were too new to this cancer game; it was all far too raw.

Justin explained that the aggressive grade-four tumour had probably been growing inside Lynda for eighteen months and the priority now was to attack the problem. Immediately. Things were moving at such a fast speed that we left with an appointment for a colonoscopy the following day. That word is something else I've come to realize the importance of.

Lynda had never had a colonoscopy, but if she'd had one at sixty, I'm pretty certain she would still be here today. In fact I am absolutely convinced. She had a private Well Woman test every year and she'd recently had a stool test. What I didn't know then, and nor did Lynda, was that a colonoscopy is the important one when it comes to detecting bowel problems.

In May 2015, I was appointed a patron of Bowel Cancer UK, and one of the messages I am hoping to get across is the importance of having a colonoscopy after fifty and every five years after that. Since all this, I've had one myself and I have already planned to have another at sixty-four. I know they're not cheap to pay for privately, but can you put a price on your life? I am also hoping to campaign for other, cheaper, screening alternatives to be made widely available.

Lynda was booked in for a scan the next day and to have a port inserted into her chest for the chemo drip. Her first session was to start on Friday.

But first we had to think how we were going to handle this news. Within the family and publicly. We talked about it on the way home. Somehow I even managed to drive us, which thinking about it now I probably wasn't really in any fit state to. Everything felt surreal; absolutely surreal. Within no time at all we'd gone from indigestion to cancer. Living to dying and back again to living with cancer. *How the hell?*

If I hadn't been around, I think Lynda would have let the world know before she did that she had the 'least sexy' cancer of them all, as she referred to it. But right from the start I was very much of the opinion that 'no, this is between you, me and family'.

In fact, I've got to be honest and say that I didn't even want her to tell the family straight away and worry them. We were being told they could control it and I wanted her to just leave it for a while. Suck it and see. But Lynda couldn't do that. Not a chance.

When we walked back into the apartment, Brad and Robbie were both there. Lynda just blurted it out to them, 'I've got cancer, but the doctor says I am not going to die.'

There's no good way at times like this, but I don't think that that was the best way they could have learnt what was going on. Both boys burst into tears, and soon we were all crying and hugging each other. The boys were full of questions and we tried, as best we could, to answer them and allay their fears. Michael came round a bit later and we had to go through it all again.

That night in bed, I was weirdly full of confidence that everything would be okay. Happy as Larry just to have heard the positive news at the end of that walk. We both were. After the shock of being brought down, we'd been lifted right back up again. Up and down like a fiddler's elbow.

'We're going to fight this; you are not going to die. You've only got twelve sessions of chemo and that will put an end to it,' I reassured her, as we held on to each other, just grateful to have been given hope.

And I truly believed it. The thought of her dying at that point never came into my mind. Or hers, I don't think.

Justin had been confident he could control it and we believed he could as well.

I wouldn't say any of this made me love Lynda any more because that just wasn't possible. I'd always loved her. But it did make me realize just how fragile life is. How everything we'd started to take for granted – our future together – might not be quite as we'd planned.

Yet I am also conscious that I am talking all the time with hindsight, which does change things. Typical of the entrepreneur in me, but I can't help thinking now: if only we could bottle and sell hindsight. What a different life we'd all be living!

But at the time it was all kicking off, we weren't thinking negatively. At all. We did not believe Lynda was going to die. We were simply going to deal with it so that it would be over and done with as soon as possible. Job done. Move on.

So, when we should have been sunning ourselves in Greece, Lynda was starting her treatment. The first people we'd told outside the family were Pat Hay and John and Angie. We had to tell John and Angie because they'd been planning to join us in Greece, but we would probably have told them anyway. Lynda and Angie went back a long way from the time their children were at school together. I obviously got to know husband and wife years later and had instantly liked them both. We trusted them with this huge secret and they never betrayed that trust.

I was adamant that otherwise Lynda should keep schtum. The showbiz world is a notoriously gossipy one and I didn't want it leaking out when we hadn't even got our own heads round it properly. We needed time. Timing is everything, Lynda used to say, when talking about acting. Not just acting, though, Babes, was it?

Had Lynda needed a further reminder of how serious cancer can be, it arrived pretty damn quickly. She woke up in hospital after her first operation, to fit the port and start her first bout of chemo, to read the news that Bernie Nolan of the Nolan Sisters had died at just fifty-two. After a long battle, breast cancer had won out in the end.

As with the boys, it wasn't the best time, if there really is ever such a thing, to hear such news and Lynda was really sad. Not for herself – even though it was a worry I think she could have done without. But she'd worked with Bernie on *The Bill* and *Calendar Girls* and had a lot of time for her. She admired her as a performer and liked her as a person.

But Lynda quickly learnt that the secret to coping with all this was not to dwell on things. If you gave in and let the negative thoughts take over, you had no chance. More than ever before, I had to be Mr Positive. So I was.

And, early on, it wasn't difficult. Not one bit. Yes it was a shock, but after that first initial fear that she was going to die, I honestly thought Lynda would be okay.

'We have to embrace it and help each other fight it,' she announced bravely when the news came out in the media within days. I'd have preferred to keep it quiet a bit longer but decisions had had to be made about cancelling the play.

The idea of not doing *A Passionate Woman* was unthinkable to Lynda. Devastating. At first, she was hoping she would be able to still perform through the chemo, if arrangements could be made for her to have it either in hospitals outside London or if the timing could be sorted to get back to London for it.

But she knew she was clutching at straws. Although she didn't get any really terrible side effects from the early chemo, she was feeling very tired and experiencing flu-like symptoms.

Performing on stage, as she knew so well, is bloody hard work, and it takes a lot of energy when you're fit and well. And even if she had been able to go ahead, there was no way the producers would be able to get her insured for a gruelling nationwide theatre tour. The decision was taken out of her hands, which was a good thing really. Lynda never could say no.

The blow was softened a bit when her long-time agent and good friend, Sue Latimer, told her that the producers still wanted her and were prepared to postpone the play for a year until she was better. But she still sobbed buckets. It was as if her whole life depended on it. It's probably hard for people going about ordinary jobs to understand this. After all, it was work, hard work. The thing most people do to pay bills, feed their families and go on holiday. But you have to remember that that wasn't the way Lynda looked at it. Work was her life. And where acting was concerned, she truly was a passionate woman.

The world had to be officially told and an announcement was made to the press, although it had been agreed that the type of cancer Lynda had would not be revealed. The last thing she wanted was to see bowel cancer 'experts' and 'survivors' sitting on a daytime TV sofa talking about what she was going through when they really didn't have a clue about her case. Everybody is different. I agreed with her completely. When we were good and ready for the story to be told, Lynda would do it herself. In her own words.

As the news about the play being postponed broke, the phones and social media went mad. Flowers, cards, texts and emails were arriving from all quarters as we tried, as best we could, to keep a low profile. Lynda admitted that it was quite a shock to realize just how loved she was by the public. That was Lynda; never one to big herself up. She did her best to answer as many letters as possible. She was still doing that right up to the end, hating to disappoint anyone.

By the end of August, though, she was sitting on the sofa of ITV's *This Morning* and telling Ruth Langsford and Eamonn Holmes, 'I'll be a new woman by Christmas!'

I was in the studio and, although it was emotional for me, I thought she would be back to full health as well. I never gave it a second thought that she wouldn't. We wouldn't allow ourselves to think any differently. Christmas was Lynda's favourite time of year and it had been ever since she was a little girl. She'd never grown out of it, although, at some point, the fun for her switched from receiving to giving presents. And boy, did she love to give. Her generosity had no end to it. Christmas had seemed such a good goal to aim for. Not too near, not too far. Just enough time to keep her going through the worst. Or so we thought.

It was the first time that Lynda had been seen on television with her new silver grey hair, and the papers went mad about it afterwards. I think they all carried a picture of the new Lynda Bellingham. Most of them also wrongly assumed that it was because of the cancer drugs, but it had nothing to do with that.

Lynda had decided that for the part of Betty in *A Passionate Woman* she really didn't want to wear a wig, which would be uncomfortable under the hot stage lighting. Yet she knew that in the era the play was set she'd probably be grey haired. So between them, she and Andrea, her hairdresser, had decided that she should go back to her natural hair colour. Neither of them had a clue what that was at the outset! She'd been dyeing it for so long.

But bleaching it lighter and lighter every fortnight for the past few months, it went back to the silvery grey colour it should have been. I really liked it, I thought it suited her. But I was also glad for her sake that she wasn't going to lose her hair, which I know must be such a hard thing for a woman. It's bad enough for a man, as I've found out myself in the last few years. Justin had told her fairly early on that the drugs wouldn't make her bald. One relief to her at least. For now, anyway. As time went on and the chemo drugs were changed, she had to wear a cold cap during the last set of treatment to prevent hair loss and her hair still thinned out.

Forced to stay at home, it was typical of Lynda to throw herself into running it like a professional housewife. Whatever she did always had to be carried out to very high standards. When she couldn't sleep at night, she'd get up to write the novel that she should have been writing in Greece. Or she'd go into the kitchen to start cooking whatever she was planning to surprise everybody with for tea. For a while it was cauliflower fritters with everything, or something that involved turmeric, cumin or cinnamon.

Determined to give herself the best possible chance of fighting cancer, she had begun researching what foods she, and we, should all eat. We were still juicing as well and for a couple of months at least it was all going well.

We'd got into a routine with the fortnightly chemo. I'd take her into Harley Street every other Friday and she'd be high as a kite for that weekend, buzzing. Unable to sleep, it was during the night that she did most of her writing.

There was no need for me to even think about having to keep her spirits up because they already were. We thought we were so lucky. I'll never forget arriving at hospital one Friday and seeing a family in the waiting room; Mum, Dad, two grown-up kids and their spouses. All six of them were crying.

We saw Justin on the way upstairs and he didn't need to or have the time to talk to us because he had bad news to deliver downstairs. I knew straight away where he was heading. Afterwards we walked out and I couldn't help looking into the waiting room, where the family still were. I felt so sorry for them. I never thought we'd ever be in the same position. And so soon.

Two days after the chemo, I'd give Lynda an injection for the white blood cells which had to be kept high to fight the cancer. We both knew that three days of flu-like symptoms would follow, but we were prepared for it and knew that would pass.

As the course went on, it got worse. Lynda started getting pins and needles, mouth ulcers and stomach cramps. But an MRI scan close to the middle of September revealed her to be a textbook case. She was responding well. Her tumour was shrinking and all the markers were good. Her first novel, *Tell Me Tomorrow*, had come out in August and had reached the bestseller list. Life was looking good.

'You never know, B, you could be doing the play after all,' I told her, full of optimism.

Then the stomach cramps began to get worse, and by the end of September the situation had changed drastically. Doing an early Christmas shoot for *Yours* magazine, she was in a lot of pain. But Lynda being Lynda, there was no way she would give anything less than a 100 per cent and she soldiered through it, smiling. And the pictures were amazing. One of me and Lynda, which is used on the jacket of this book, we had copied and printed to send out as Christmas cards. The original we had framed and hung it on the lounge wall. And they say the camera never lies!

After the shoot, Lynda had to resort to taking a morphine tablet given to her in case of emergencies. And on our way to Harley Street for her chemo early the next morning, she felt so rough that she had to take a bucket with her in the car in case she was sick. Typical Lynda, she held it back until we arrived and then raced straight off to the loo to throw up in there.

When I asked her why she didn't use the bucket, she said that she didn't want to make a mess in the car or a fuss. Did she ever just think of herself? No is the answer.

Within half an hour, her chemo was cancelled and she was hooked up to various drips, but she was still in terrible pain with the stomach cramps and her blood pressure was high. By Monday she was well enough to have the chemo while the duty doctor explained that the cramps were the body's way of fighting the chemo. Nonetheless, her tumour was shrinking. We arrived home reassured once more.

But by early December, when she should have been finishing her treatment, things were looking very dodgy indeed. Her tumour markers were up which meant that the chemo was no longer working, and it was clear she'd need a different cocktail. We learnt too that she would need to be on chemo for the rest of her life.

After a particularly rough weekend, when she was in a lot of pain from the cramps, I took one look at her on the Monday morning and said, 'I think we'd better get you in.'

By now Justin had started listening to me when he asked Lynda how she was, because he knew I'd tell him the truth. Lynda always tried to be so positive and cheerful. She could be her own worst enemy with that attitude.

It was obvious, despite her brave face, that she was in

considerable pain. I hated seeing her suffer, so I begged Justin to take her in there and then. Although Lynda didn't like it one bit, he agreed.

Taking me to one side, Justin explained that Lynda was going have to have an operation to insert a stent and open up her colon, which was being blocked by the tumour and stopping food passing through. The blockage was causing the stomach cramps.

I'll never forget the date because it was Friday the 13th when Lynda had to have her operation. While she was being prepared by the nurses, the surgeon was looking at the latest scan results. He admitted that he really didn't know if they could do what they wanted to.

'Do your best,' I told him and she went in. But not long afterwards I was sitting in the waiting room when the oldest of the regular nurses came in and asked me to go with her.

I followed to find Lynda was being wheeled back out of the theatre. The anaesthetist explained that they needed to do an emergency operation to remove the tumour within the next half an hour or so or she would die. And they needed Richard Cohen to do it.

I was in bits, absolute bits, when Richard came running through the door. The nurses were lined up ready. Lynda was drifting in and out of consciousness as she signed the consent form. I signed another and Richard was running out of another door, telling me he'd have her down to the basement theatre in half an hour.

As we waited for them to be ready, I held her hand and cried my eyes out. The nurses kept coming over to give me a hug. When the porters arrived, I stayed with her until the automatic theatre doors opened. All I could see were people in there running round like headless chickens. The doors closed on me and I stood there all alone and just sobbed and sobbed. It felt like an hour, although it was probably only four or five minutes, before I thought, *What do I do? Where do I go?*

So I took the lift up to the foyer, where the guys on the front desk told me to wait in the critical care unit. I did as I was told and paced up and down there for hours. I think I phoned John and Angie, Nickolas and Biggins, but I'm not sure. They all said they were coming straight to the hospital but I stopped them. I didn't want anybody with me. I can't explain it, but the last thing I needed was somebody speaking into my left ear, however sympathetically, saying everything is going to be okay. When, deep down in my heart, I didn't think I would ever see her alive again.

At 10 p.m., Richard arrived, still with his scrubs on, and I burst out crying. 'Stop crying, she's alive!' he told me and we sat down to talk.

'How did it go?' was the first question. He explained

that it had gone well, but he could see secondaries in the liver. The tumour he'd removed had been as big as his fist and he'd had to give her a stoma, which is an opening made on the abdomen to allow food waste – usually liquid – to pass out. A changeable bag is attached to hold it.

'How long has she got?' I asked, fearing the worst, and he said he reckoned about two.

'Are we talking weeks or months?'

No, years, it turned out, and I gave him the biggest hug as I sobbed, 'Thank you.'

I was just so grateful she was still alive. Richard left me sitting in the room on my own, thinking: *Great, I've got her back*. We had another two years and, by that time, medical science might well have moved on and they might have found a cure for her vicious cancer.

Suddenly it dawned on me that I hadn't eaten a thing all day. In the waiting room somebody had left a yellow Selfridges bag with empty sandwich wrappers, but also an untouched bar of Cadbury's chocolate. I wolfed it down.

When the nurses came to tell me she was fetching Lynda up, she warned me not to be surprised; there would be a lot of tubes. Half an hour later the lift doors opened and Lynda was wheeled out awake. I have never seen so many tubes on anybody in my life but I was just so happy to see her alive.

Grabbing her arm, I asked, 'How are you feeling, B?'

'Like shit!' was the answer.

Say it as it is, Babes. We were both good at that!

Soon it was 1.30 in the morning and the nurse was telling me that Lynda needed to sleep, so we said our good-byes.

I'll never forget that just as I was walking out through the door, she called out from beneath all the tubes, 'Michael, remember there's loads of stuff in the freezer so don't go hungry.'

Who else, who else would have been thinking like that at such a time?

I looked back, shook my head and said, 'Nothing changes.' That was my woman!

I was still laughing to myself when I got into the lift. A few hours earlier I really thought she'd gone. I cannot even start to describe the relief I was feeling. I was over the moon. We now had another two years! And, right there and then, it felt like a lifetime in front of us. A future again.

By eleven the next morning I was back at her bedside, where I stayed until mid-afternoon when she told me to do her a favour.

'Don't come back tonight,' she instructed.

'Why not?' I wanted to know, baffled.

'I feel I need to entertain you,' she added. No good at all me telling her she didn't need to. Lynda always felt she had to entertain anybody in her presence. Responsible for everyone, even in her own bloody hour of need.

The last thing I felt was in a party mood, but I'd promised Lynda that I would go to her sister Jean's Christmas do that Sunday afternoon, as we'd planned, and I'd take the boys. Leaving Jean's house at about 4 p.m., I headed back to hospital and, as I got into the lift, I bumped into Justin.

I'll never forget him telling me, 'I always reckon my patients have three lives and Lynda has just had one.'

It was then that he mentioned putting her on a new trial drug. I bowed to his knowledge and we headed off to put the idea to her. I'll never forget seeing her face as we walked in together and the fear in her expression. She looked like a rabbit trapped in the headlights. She was absolutely frightened to death.

'What's up?' she wanted to know.

'Everything's fine, Babes. You're doing well,' I reassured her.

She admitted later that she'd thought we'd come to tell her she was going to die.

When Justin left, Lynda asked me if I wanted to see her stoma. Trust her! I really don't like blood or needles so I declined as politely as I could, and we were just sitting talking when Richard Cohen arrived to check on his handiwork. Whether I liked it or not, I was about to see the results of his plumbing as well. Suddenly you wise up. This was the woman I love and I needed to support her now in a very practical way.

And if that meant changing stoma bags when the effects of the op kicked in, so be it. It had never bothered me changing Brad and Stacey's nappies when they were little. I can't say it was ever at the top of my list of the best things to do, but I got on with it. I needed to adopt the same attitude now. Under the expert guidance of Becky, the specialist stoma nurse, I started to learn what to do. Lynda wasn't happy about it but she couldn't do it herself right now. Again, because I loved her so much, it really didn't bother me. I am a practical man, and it is only poo at the end of the day. You just do it.

It was harder for Lynda, though, and she felt belittled.

'You shouldn't be doing this,' she kept saying and I kept telling her it didn't matter. Besides, if everything went well she'd be able to have it reversed a few months down the line. There was always hope.

By now we both had to accept that she'd been a bit too optimistic back in August when she vowed to be a new woman by Christmas.

'I realize now I was in shock and denial for the first few months,' she admitted. 'I don't think I quite understood . . .'

She'd been looking forward to Christmas so much and wanted it all to be absolutely perfect. She'd been away in panto for the previous two years and 2013 had been – in her words nicked from the Queen – her *annus horribilis*.

Straight talking as ever, Lynda told journalists, 'This Christmas is very precious to me because I'm still here!'

Now, much as I keep saying I am a practical man, who could build you a house blindfolded, there's one thing I really cannot do and that's cook. So Christmas dinner was always going to be a real challenge without Lynda. But I like a challenge and I was willing to have a go under her very detailed written instructions. Stacey offered to do it, but I was adamant that I'd have a go myself.

Of course Lynda had been planning it for weeks. The organic turkey had been ordered, a kitchen cupboard had been stuffed with every snack imaginable: Twiglets, chocolate, cashew nuts, Turkish delight, and there were presents for stockings for the boys in a box at the bottom of our bed.

She'd even organized and got the family to club together for a joint present for me – another Harris tweed jacket I'd spotted in the window of a tailor's shop next door to the dentist's. I always liked to buy her jewellery.

On Christmas Eve, I peeled the spuds and sprouts with the help of our regular cleaners – Julia and her mum – who took pity on me! Michael managed to get back from Wolverhampton, where he was appearing in panto, and we went to midnight Mass together at St Stephen Walbrook, where we both prayed that Lynda would soon be well enough to come home.

When we all visited her in hospital on Christmas morning, she was heartbroken not to be celebrating with us all, but there was no chance. She just wasn't well enough and she knew it. I used to joke that she was becoming institutionalized. But when she was allowed home a week later, even she was frightened to leave hospital, with the nurses and carers always on hand. I tried to do my best, and I don't think all in all that I was a bad nurse, but I was no expert.

Leaving her early afternoon, I drove home to tackle the Christmas turkey, which cooked more quickly than it should have done so the spuds weren't quite roasted. All the while, texts and photos were flying backwards and forwards from Lynda's hospital bedside to the kitchen. Let's just say, it wasn't the best Christmas dinner we'd ever eaten. Okay, maybe it was the worst. But everybody ate it and you can't argue with that!

Now I think if only we'd known it would be Lynda's last Christmas, I'd have definitely organized things differently. Don't ask me exactly how. Just somehow . . .

CHAPTER 9

THE SECRET'S OUT

......

It's early evening on New Year's Eve, 2013, and Lynda is lying in her own king-sized bed in her own home. For that she is grateful, but anxious at the same time. And who can blame her? She's just had a major lifesaving operation and is feeling like death warmed up. Her body is not working the same as it was before the emergency op and while she's made jokes about shit happening when you least expect it, it's only been to mask the underlying worry. She's not fooling her full-time nurse: me! Michael Pattemore TLC. No wonder she's feeling nervous . . .

To take her mind – and mine – off her complicated medical condition, I put myself in charge of entertainment. Let's face it, neither of us is going to be partying with the rest of the world tonight. Those crowds on Sydney Harbour are going to have to watch the fireworks – something we've always wanted to do – without us for another year.

But hey, it's not all bad. We've been given two more years so for now at least we can put that worry away in a box and carry on living from day to day the very best we can. Besides, we've just been able to reveal another, much better, secret that we've been keeping up our sleeves to set the New Year off with a real bang.

A good few weeks ago, the nice guy Stuart who has delivered our registered post since we moved in here rang the doorbell and was standing on the landing with a specially franked, expensive looking-parchment envelope. I could see it was addressed to Lynda and I was immediately intrigued.

Going back inside I'd handed it to her, hoping it would be what I suspected. And it was! Her face was a picture as she read the official letter from the Cabinet Office informing her that she was being awarded an OBE in the New Year's Honours List for her charity work. That letter, as well as a second one from Charles and Camilla congratulating her, is now framed and hanging on the wall of the lounge above a side table. I find myself looking at it often and, even now, it makes me burst with pride.

Now Lynda was very patriotic and a great fan of the royals, so she was understandably over the moon. And absolutely bursting to tell everyone. But if there had been anything remotely positive about these recent months, they had at least taught her that it was possible for her to keep a secret.

At Christmas, she'd wanted to share her good news with the family but I'd persuaded her not to. 'They won't give it to you if the news gets out, girl,' I warned, and she was scared enough by that thought to listen to what I was saying.

But now, New Year's Eve, it was about to be out in the open, and if ever there was a right time for Lynda to be recognized for the years and years of relentless, unpaid charity work she'd so readily undertaken, it was now. Thank you God. The other person to thank was Katie Mallalieu, a teaching assistant from Lancashire who had befriended Lynda on Twitter and nominated her. The two had worked together on a couple of fundraising projects for the Alzheimer's Society.

It was the bright spark on the horizon that Lynda definitely needed. Something to celebrate for a change, though at the time of her operation she feared she might not live to collect it.

Grabbing hold of my hand when she was in so much pain hours before going down to theatre, she'd gasped: 'I don't think I will be here to pick up my OBE. You'll have to collect it for me.' I, of course, burst out crying and told her, 'Don't be so stupid,' all the while praying she was going to be proved wrong. That day and the pain she was in will haunt me for the rest of my life.

Yet, mercifully, here she still was. To celebrate, I opened the usual New Year's Eve bottle of champagne and, although Lynda could only manage a sip or two, we toasted her gong which would be officially announced in all the papers the following day. In my role as entertainment coordinator, I'd opened all the wooden shutters on our bedroom windows and we lay there, just happy to be in each other's arms, watching the huge firework display light up the sky from Ally Pally, aka the People's Palace and Alexandra Palace, which originally opened for the nation on Queen Victoria's fifty-fourth birthday. And remember how Lynda loved fireworks.

Afterwards we started watching one of Lynda's favourite films, *The Godfather*, on Sky movies, but by around three in the morning we were both nodding off so we recorded the last bit and settled down to sleep.

The following day, the phone went mad with friends and colleagues congratulating Lynda and reporters desperate for more details but, anxious not to give too much away about her illness in her excitement, she spoke only to one or two.

Before the official ceremony in March, there was of course the question of the Palace Outfit. Now nobody loved shopping like Lynda and she was a woman on a mission. Of course she had to be practical because of Furby – the name she'd christened her stoma. Nothing too figure-hugging. A trip to the usual West End department stores with Jean proved useless. Even John Lewis let her down on this occasion, and it took a call to her hairdressers to point her in the direction of a designer dress shop near Marble Arch.

She was like a child walking into a sweet shop and she found just what she wanted: a navy blue dress and an ivory coat. The navy blue fascinator she wore to Helen Worth's wedding and a pair of handmade ivory suede shoes finished off the outfit. Sod the expense as long as she was happy and fit for royalty!

I've been to two garden parties at Buckingham Palace with Lynda and this was my third trip there. And I loved it, I absolutely loved it. For someone who has been to prison, to drive their Range Rover through those famous gates and under that historic archway in the courtyard and park in the quadrangle round the back, is phenomenal. You have got no idea until it happens to you. And then to be there with Lynda receiving an OBE was something else altogether.

We'd received three tickets, but Lynda phoned up and asked for an extra one so all three boys were with us: Michael, Robbie and Bradley. When I look back now, we probably could have got another and Stacey could have come as well, but at the time we didn't dare push it. As Brad was living with us he'd have felt the most excluded if he hadn't been there.

So it was just me and the boys, all suited and booted, and Lynda looking a million dollars on the big day. And what a day. The sun shone, everybody was proud and happy. When we arrived inside Buckingham Palace, we were ushered upstairs to the ballroom where the ceremony was to take place. Lynda went off into another room. Then when everybody was in place, all the people receiving their medals filed in together in front of us. As their names were called, they went forwards and curtseyed or bowed to the royal family member doing the honours. Everything worked like clockwork.

Lynda did tell us afterwards that she got a slight ticking off by a man in a uniform for leaving her place in her own group to go and chat to Katherine Jenkins, who like Lynda was there to receive an OBE for her charity work, and also her music. Katherine had introduced herself to Lynda when they were doing *Strictly* and told her that she'd bought Lynda's old house in Muswell Hill from the people who bought it from Lynda. Small world and all that.

During the official bit, Lynda had a nice chat with Prince Charles who was performing the honours as Her Majesty the Queen had another engagement.

After telling her how lovely it was to see her there,

Charles wanted to know how she found time for all her charity work. Typical Lynda, she joked that she was covering all bases, meaning should she ever find herself in need of any of the services offered by all the charities she supported, she could rest assured she'd done her bit to help them. Apparently he laughed and appreciated it when she made the point that her OBE would help her raise money and awareness for his PRIME charity.

It was a beautiful ceremony and did I feel proud of Lynda? Just a bit! Did I cry? Just a bit! Bless her heart.

Of course, Furby kept Lynda's feet – or should I say hand and knees – firmly on the ground. That's the position she ended up in kneeling over the loo basin at Buckingham Palace emptying her stoma bag – a task she'd got down to a fine art involving a series of jugs so not to make a mess between bag and basin. Now some people might find that embarrassing and humiliating, but Lynda saw the funny side. She was never one to be beaten. She always drilled in to the boys how important it was to stay positive. Her favourite expression was: 'palms up; heads to the sky'. I think it ended with something like 'and don't let the bastards grind you down' which makes her sound a bit cynical, but she wasn't. She always made a big deal of being nice to people.

After leaving the Palace, we headed for the Delaunay restaurant in the Aldwych, where we'd reserved a private room for a celebration lunch with some of our family and friends, including Katie Mallalieu who'd done all the hard work completing the mass of paperwork to get Lynda the OBE. The wine and champagne flowed and it turned out to be quite an emotional do. I made a speech, Lynda made a speech and of course Biggins made a speech.

It was a day to remember for the rest of our lives – no matter how long or short that might be. By 7 p.m., though, Lynda was tucked up in bed, where she slept like a log all night. Initially I think she was a bit miffed with me for going to the pub in the evening with John and Angie. Maybe I shouldn't have carried on partying without her, but I knew she'd be fast asleep in no time and I'd be on my own again as the boys had all gone out. Sometimes, I needed a blowout. It could be hard work staying so positive when, underneath, we both knew she was so ill. But although she tried to warn us that she wouldn't be around for too much longer, we refused to give up hope. And while ever there was hope, there was life.

For the second time that day, though, she'd had to sort out Furby, who'd reacted badly to a few glasses of wine and for once it got to her that she'd never be in control of her own body again. When I arrived back, I hadn't wanted to disturb her so I'd slept on the sofa, where she found me the next morning. She'd forgiven me by then as she understood that I needed a break sometimes, especially as I was often struggling to sleep at night.

One thing I'd been getting into the habit of after her operation in December was sleeping with one eye half open. Just in case she needed anything in the night. A glass of water, painkiller, a reassuring cuddle, moral support . . . Somehow it was always easier to be positive in the daytime. Nights could be lonely and full of fear.

Lynda always had a soft spot for carers and I was starting to properly understand why. I seem to remember that she was involved in promoting Carers' Week in 2013 and she appeared on ITV's *Lorraine* to talk about it. She always genuinely believed they were an unsung bunch of heroes doing a very difficult job, often in isolation. They save the government millions of pounds each year, she used to say, for doing such a vital job of looking after sick, elderly and disabled family and friends.

At the very end of her life, Lynda talked about how she wished she was here for longer so she could do more to champion their cause. In her view (and now mine), caring should be promoted more to young people as a proper, worthwhile profession. Lynda knew she couldn't manage without them herself at that time. Professional carers and otherwise – even me!

*

The next highlight between chemotherapy and hospital visits was a trip at the end of May to Lake Como for Lynda's sixty-sixth birthday and our sixth wedding anniversary. It was around the same time that the news of George Clooney's engagement to the glamorous barrister Amal Alamuddin had broken. Clooney had a home in Lake Como and Lynda had been hoping to catch a glimpse of him – in time for him to change his mind and marry her, she joked! Eventually she accepted that she already had Mr Spain and was being greedy wanting Mr Italy (or Mr Hollywood) as well!

Sue Latimer and her husband Edward joined us on Lynda's actual birthday and anniversary, and we'd had lunch and dinner together. Sue surprised Lynda with a handbag she said she liked in a local shop, close to where we were staying, and I bought her a couple of necklaces she chose in another. She always loved to wear big, modern chunky necklaces. Luckily she spoke fairly fluent Italian which always made things easier whenever we went shopping or eating out.

Back home, her VIP star was still rising. Hot on the heels of her OBE, in June, Lynda was decorated with a Fellowship from the University of Worcester when she officially opened the National Centre for the Study and Prevention of Violence and Abuse. Once again she was thrilled.

As with all her life experiences, Lynda had always been keen to turn her own sorry saga of domestic abuse into something positive, and she used to give lectures to Worcestershire police on how to train their officers to deal with it. Behind closed doors, she could talk openly and honestly to explain that domestic abuse is not always about drunken husbands beating up their wives, it is as much about mental abuse as anything else. I went with her to several lectures and on many occasions she got a standing ovation. But she was always there in her own time, for no pay, never for the glory. She just wanted to save other women from the trauma she'd been through. That was Lynda all over.

At one of Lynda's charity events, I'll never forget meeting one lady who had been married to a solicitor – he'd been mentally abusing her for years before she'd found the courage to leave him. Solicitors and doctors can be abusers just as well as unemployed labourers on benefits. It's a problem that crosses all social boundaries and affects people from all walks of life. I know that Lynda would have been saddened, as I was, to learn that Star Support & Counselling, a charity of which she was a patron, had folded a few months after her death because of a lack of funding.

Between these exciting ceremonies, though, life went on in the same mundane fashion. Lynda carried on cooking – even when she often couldn't eat any of it herself. She also became addicted to the reality television show *Come Dine with Me.* She was fascinated by how deluded a lot of the dinner party cooks were about their abilities in the kitchen. While she'd never consider herself an expert cook, she knew she could lick them all if it came to it. Too right she could.

All in all, the cancer worry aside, I can't really say it was a miserable time. When she wasn't cooking, cleaning, shopping at Waitrose or watching daytime television, Lynda was glued to her computer keyboard writing. She'd completed her second novel, *The Boy I Love,* and was now writing her second autobiography, *There's Something I've Been Dying to Tell You.*

She'd wanted to bring the subject of death out in the open for a long time, way before she was ill, but when she pitched the idea of doing a show about it to television bosses, it had been dismissed as being too depressing.

She felt frustrated by their reaction as she knew it didn't have to be that way. Much as she liked and admired Billy Connolly as an entertainer (he used to hold court at Wednesday evening cocktail parties at the Athenaeum), she felt he hadn't really done the subject justice in his *Big Send Off* documentary about dealing with death.

Her argument was that the way modern medicine was keeping us alive for so much longer, it naturally followed that the way we die – and our attitude towards it – had to change to catch up. Never in a million years did we think when we first discussed this that she'd be in this position herself quite so soon. In fact, when she was writing the book, I'd come home in sometimes and find her slumped over the keyboard. Thankfully, she'd have only fallen fast asleep from exhaustion, but there were times when I thought I'd lost her for good.

Lynda's biggest fear was Alzheimer's as she'd seen her adoptive mother, Ruth, face a long struggle with the disease that started when she suddenly forgot how to use the washing machine. Her father, too, had mild dementia before he died. One of his great joys after Ruth went into a home was going into Tesco's for a big fried breakfast when he did his weekly shop. But one day Lynda's sister Barbara, who lived near Don, got a phone call from a woman who worked there saying he'd just gone in for a second breakfast without realizing he'd just had one. It saddened her beyond belief that her father, a former wartime bomber pilot, had been reduced to this.

Then the following year, Lynda learnt that her birth mother Marjorie also had the condition. It was that biological link that really brought it home to her that she might be vulnerable.

Of course it was the effect it would have on her acting that panicked her most, mainly learning her lines. She had friends of an age who had lost their nerve because their memory wasn't what it was. Once the fear took a grip, it became self-perpetuating and they didn't perform on stage ever again.

So far, though, if Lynda ever forgot a word on stage, her brain had always filled in the gap and found a substitute without the audience guessing anything at all. As long as that happened, she felt reassured. She'd told us all that if it ever looked like her mind had started to deteriorate, she wanted to go into care without any of us feeling guilty about it. And once she reached the stage of not knowing who, what or where, she'd rather die than be left merely to exist. She wanted to be taken to the Dignitas clinic.

'Please, please, please take me,' she'd beg. Again, I find myself asking the question, *Would I?*

If you'd asked me that question ten years ago, I would have looked round and said: 'No way, José!' But now, knowing that I am getting older myself, and after seeing Lynda in so much pain with cancer, my mind has changed completely and I think the answer would have to be yes. I do think that's hard for people who have never seen someone terminally ill to try and understand this.

But I am also aware that until the time actually comes, we cannot ever really know.

*

One thing I did know, but had kept to myself for quite a while, was that Lynda would never be able to work as an actress again. It was becoming more and more obvious, however much I wanted to believe otherwise for her sake.

By the time of my fifty-ninth birthday on Sunday, 18 August, the end was already in sight. Me and Lynda both knew that it would be the last one we'd spend together and she was determined to surprise me with a huge party at home. She'd organized everything and invited thirty or forty people to celebrate with us.

But on Friday, 16th, when she went for her chemo, she'd been dehydrated and had to stay in hospital under doctor's orders. She was devastated. For Lynda's sake as much as mine, I suspect, family stepped in to take me out for lunch instead at Côte Brasserie in Highgate. Afterwards, we all came home for coffee and cake and Lynda managed to join in singing 'Happy Birthday' via a mobile video call from her hospital bed. Much as she loved her old fashioned quill and her diary, she couldn't fault new technology during these months!

She laughed to see me with Jean's present – a giant wine glass that holds vast amounts so that I could truthfully tell the doctor I only have one glass of red a day!

Underneath the jolly front and the brave faces, however, we knew we were running out of time fast. Lynda had been on borrowed time since Christmas, and she was now slipping away from me; we all knew it. Up to the beginning of August, everything seemed under control. There'd been hints back in March from her frontline carers that perhaps it was a good time to put her affairs in order. And she could see in Justin's eyes that it was getting harder for him to be positive. The chemo was getting stronger but becoming less effective, and she wasn't suitable for trial drugs.

It was at the beginning of August that Lynda really started to suffer with the effects of the chemo. Her mouth was so sore and full of ulcers that she couldn't eat anything, and her throat was sore with thrush. That famously sexy voice was fading and that really saddened her. It had been her professional trademark for so long. The palms of her hands had turned black and she was in constant pain. Her stoma was bleeding and sore, and all in all it was hell for her.

'I think we need to see Richard Cohen ...' I told her looking at her one day and she agreed. So there we were on 12 August – the Glorious Twelfth, the start of the grouse season as she referred to it – sitting opposite her surgeon and being told that the chemo was now killing her as much as the cancer. We already knew that she wasn't suitable for trial drugs and we also knew that even the dumbest cancer cells can outwit the brightest oncologist. It wasn't looking good.

Richard wanted us to see the oncologist so off we went to speak to Justin Stebbing about an hour later. As blunt as ever, Lynda sat there and asked him, 'Is it time for me to fall off the twig?' He replied no, not quite. Her next question was, 'Can you get me to Christmas?'

He didn't actually say no, but I knew from the look on his face that that wasn't going to happen. Deep down, I think Lynda did too.

'If you can get me to Christmas, I'll come off the chemo at the end of November and then slip away at the end of January,' she announced. We already knew that if she stopped the chemo altogether, she'd probably have eight weeks to live.

The original plan had always been to shrink the tumour and undergo another operation to take out the secondaries and stoma and reconnect the bowel. But in order to do that, Lynda would have to curtail chemo for the operation. It was obvious that that was now completely out of the question.

Suddenly, it was all happening a bit too fast for me, and I had to butt in and ask what would happen if her condition improved. While Justin reassured me the chemo could be restarted at any time, his face was telling me that would not be happening.

We'd already talked about stopping treatment when the time came. But if you'd asked me would I ever want Lynda to give up the chemo at the start of all this, I would have definitely said: 'No, I want you here to the very end.'

But, by this point, I could not do it. I realized without a shadow of a doubt that I was just being selfish wanting her here at any cost; you wouldn't even do that to a dog. This is when you realize it is not about you, it is about the person who has got the cancer. They are the ones suffering and you have no right to demand they put up with the pain just to hang on a little bit longer to please you and spare your own pain.

Now, here's what I'd like to explain properly. It was never Lynda's decision in the end when to die. Justin had agreed that the chemo would be cut back by half now, to give her back some quality of life, and it would be stopped – as she wished – in November. And that, as far as we were aware, was the plan. We just never got that far . . .

So after the decision was made, the chemo was cut back and within a couple of weeks, Lynda's quality of life was so much better. The ulcers disappeared and she had bags more energy; her old sparkle was back. She was buzzing again.

We arranged a holiday to Corfu and carried on planning Christmas and persuading ourselves that her life wasn't going to end any time before then. Cancer would absolutely not spoil that.

Unable to get out to the shops and not being an internet shopper, Lynda had taken to ordering things from catalogues. All the while, the unspoken question was there: would she get her money's worth out of it before . . .

It was like that when we ordered some new dining chairs. The set we already had looked fantastic, all white leather and chrome, but being high backed they were top heavy. It was a real design fault. Whenever anybody got up off one, it would topple over, and it used to drive Lynda mad.

By now, she was planning her perfect last Christmas with a huge proper tree and all the trimmings. For once she knew her limitations and, reluctantly, she'd already accepted that she wouldn't attempt to do the cooking herself. The plan was to go to a hotel for dinner, then come back and have pudding and presents at home. She planned to shop for the stockings in November.

'Then I've done everything I set out to do,' she'd say. 'The good thing about dying like this is that you can plan.'

Oh, Babes. If only we didn't have to make these plans . . .

She'd seen a television advert for Furniture Village and had spotted just the set of dining chairs she wanted for us all to sit down on for our Christmas pud. So one Friday after chemo, we'd gone down there to order a set of twelve. My heart sank when I heard there was a three-month wait as they had to come from Italy, but the assistant assured us we'd have them before Christmas.

While I refused to take that hope away from Lynda, I was starting to have my serious doubts about whether she'd make it. Deep down, I knew the answer and it was not the one I wanted it to be.

But first, we had to enjoy a little sunshine. The two of us were going to Corfu, then she wanted to take the boys to Tenerife for one last blast.

Although she was unable to get travel insurance, Lynda was far too concerned about creating lasting memories for us all to bother about the practicalities of her condition.

'As long as I'm near an airport and can take a swig of morphine and jump on a flight back quickly, I refuse to worry,' she'd say.

So in the middle of September we flew out to the Marbella Corfu Hotel and Spa for what was to be our last holiday together. On drastically reduced doses of chemotherapy, Lynda was back to her old self and we had a lovely time chatting to the other guests, many of whom were fans of Lynda's. One, a nurse from Inverness called Kerry, became a fantastic support to have around both practically and morally. She was in charge of a surgical ward back at home and she made Lynda feel safe. I was extremely grateful to her for that. Kerry's mother-in-law, Jean, was a fan of Lynda's and we all had a selfie taken together and texted it to her.

We were supposed to be choosing the hymns for Lynda's funeral during the twelve days we were away, but because we were having such a lovely time I didn't have the heart to bring the subject up.

Lynda was determined to talk about what I'd do after she'd gone. 'When I finally do die, you need to go away,' she ordered in her best bossy Oxo mum voice. Glass of wine in my hand, I just murmured non-committedly, 'We'll see.'

'I think you should, you're going to have to keep busy. You can't sit at home all day long. I'll tell you what: let's go and book it.'

I looked at her and said, 'Have you got a direct line to God or something? How can we book it when we don't know when it's going to happen?'

At that we both started to laugh, she dropped the subject, and we enjoyed the rest of our stay. There was one scary morning when her legs – so skinny by now – gave way and she fell down in the bathroom. That's when I knew things were not going well . . .

She always liked to get up very early to watch the sun rise from the balcony, but first she had to empty her stoma bag. This particular morning, I woke up to the sound of a loud clunk and a bang coming from the bathroom.

Jumping out of bed, I found her in a right old state. The bag had filled to overflowing during the night and by the time she made it out of bed to the bathroom, it had come away and exploded all over herself and the floor. Completely naked, she was crying and trying to clean up the mess. That's the problem with stomas; you have no control over them at all. And Lynda especially liked to be in control.

She was really upset when I walked in and found her like that. She felt so belittled; it was so undignified.

For once, though, she didn't put up too much of a fight and try to argue 'I can do it myself' as I grabbed the towels and started to clean up. It wasn't the nicest job in the world, but it didn't bother me one bit except to see her so upset at losing her dignity. She was in terrible pain, terrible. Picking her up, I lay her down on a towel on the bed; washed and dressed her in her swimming costume. As soon as I'd got her settled on the balcony, I rang down to reception for clean towels and then phoned her cancer nurse back at the London Oncology Clinic to discuss the collapse. It wasn't the only time it had happened, as she'd already fallen down the hotel staircase and landed in a heap on the reception floor. After checking with the doctor she rang back and told me to up her morphine dose by an extra 50mg.

By mid-morning, Lynda wanted a sleep so I went

downstairs and sat outside with a newspaper and beer. With my sunglasses on, I didn't think anyone could see when I started to cry, but suddenly I felt the hand of our nice waitress, Anna Maria, on my back.

'Why are you crying?' she asked and I blurted out, 'My wife is dying.' Bless her heart, Anna Maria burst out crying as well, recalling how her father had died of cancer several years ago.

That evening, we'd gone down to the restaurant for lobster night. I love lobster and so did Lynda. All the waiters and waitresses came over to give her a hug; Anna Maria must have told them. That was when I knew for certain that there was not going to be any miracle; Lynda was not going to make Christmas. And we couldn't pretend otherwise for much longer.

The following day we flew home to prepare for the media storm Lynda's memoir was going to create. The press had been gagging for information and soon they'd have what they wanted.

I'd arranged for wheelchair assistance when we arrived at Gatwick, knowing she'd never make the walk from the arrivals lounge to a car.

Looking round at me, she said, resigned, 'Tenerife's out, isn't it?' I had to agree, but we decided to go with the boys to the five star hotel The Grove, in Hertfordshire, for a last luxury weekend instead. Sadly we didn't even make it that far.

At Lynda's insistence, I was in Italy meeting up with my old friends Richard and Shannon from the States for a few days when the news broke. It was Sunday, 28 September, and the *Mail on Sunday* had run the first serialization of Lynda's memoir, *There's Something I've Been Dying to Tell You*.

The secret was out. Lynda Bellingham OBE was dying of bowel cancer.

CHAPTER 10

GOODBYE AND GOD BLESS X

······

It is midday on Wednesday, 15 October, and I am sitting at Lynda's hospital bedside when she suddenly grabs hold of me and starts sobbing, 'Michael, I don't want to die.'

It is the first time she has ever said it outright and it comes as a real shock. (It will be the only time she said it, too.) I cannot think of a single word to say because there just aren't any, any more. None exist. So I choke back my own tears and just hold my very brave, very sick wife tight, kissing her over and over again as she lies there looking terrified. Somehow, she must have known herself in that moment that her days, not weeks or months any more, were now numbered. Of that I am convinced. Absolutely convinced.

Yet, only a week beforehand, she was smiling for the

cameras as she gave confident television, radio, newspaper and magazine interviews insisting that she was not frightened of dying and arguing that nobody could expect to live for ever. She'd ignored her pain and travelled to Manchester by train in bright pink high heels to appear on *BBC Breakfast* and tell the waiting nation that her decision to stop chemo was a huge relief because she'd taken back some control of herself and her life.

'I don't want the boys or my husband to see me die a little sad old lady. I want to go out there as I am,' she announced with such courage and dignity.

And she meant every single word of it. By now of course she was the nation's darling. She'd long been a goddess and a national treasure, but now she was a saint in the public's opinion. Everybody had been struck by her honesty and bravery, and she was determined not to disappoint or let them down in any way. Taking full advantage of her status, she was putting on the performance of her life in the hope that her own strength, when staring death in the face, would help and inspire other people in her position to do the same. Duty to others always came first with Lynda. Always.

'If, by telling my story, I have helped just one terminally ill person face up to the inevitable, it will have been worthwhile. That may mean choosing when to stop failing chemotherapy treatment, as I have, or it could mean preparing husbands, wives, children, friends emotionally or practically,' she explained.

Yet, whether you liked it or not, B, you were only human at the end of the day – and just as vulnerable as the rest of us underneath it all. You had every right to want to stay alive and be shit scared of dying. Who wouldn't be? You didn't want to leave me alone or leave the boys without seeing them settled down. Or leave your remaining family, especially Jean, the last surviving Bellingham sister. Or your many friends, beloved fans and the profession you loved so much. Who the hell in their right mind would?

Nobody could blame Lynda for finally letting the mask slip and admit it as she was doing that day. The bizarre thing was that even though my head must have also known she was about to leave me, as I tried to comfort her in her hour of need, my heart still couldn't quite believe she would. I know, it doesn't really make sense, but that is the best way I can describe it. Perhaps that's what happens to everyone in this position. You can't ever give up hope because it is as if you are letting the person down if you do; wishing them away somehow. As if I had any bloody influence in the matter . . .

When the news first came out, all the public attention was quite overwhelming for her. More than overwhelming, in fact. She was genuinely shocked. This was the woman who didn't think anybody would travel to her funeral and nor would she expect them to when it was going to be held so far out of London, so to spare them the time and guilt, she'd planned a second knees up in the city. Honestly!

To be fair, though, as much as I knew she was loved, even I hadn't realized just how much. It hit me as soon as I arrived back from Italy on the Monday, twenty-four hours after that first headline in the *Mail on Sunday*. We'd spent most of the day on the phone to each other and I'd told her not to answer any calls; just to lie low and I'd deal with them when I got back.

She'd been purposely keeping a very low profile for the past few months. The real reason we hadn't gone to Denise Welch's wedding to the publicist Lincoln Townley in Portugal in July had been because as soon as Lynda had walked in, people would have taken one look at her and known there was something seriously wrong. Neither of us had wanted to risk that.

Only a small handful of people had known the type of cancer Lynda had and that it was terminal, so of course the show business fraternity went mad when she came clean. Everybody was shocked and wanting to send messages of love and support. The home phone, Lynda's mobile, my mobile went mad. Absolutely mad. There was no way we could answer them all even if we'd wanted. Twitter and other social media and newspaper websites had gone into overdrive. It was a right old storm. Hundreds more sympathy cards flooded in and flowers started arriving by the bucketful.

Forced to prioritize the shocked calls, I rang people like Biggins, Nickolas Grace, Lesley Joseph, Lynda La Plante and the *Loose Women* to tell them the sad, sorry score. Yes, it really was true. Yes, my lovely Lynda was dying. Well, that was what we'd been told anyway . . .

Somehow, she still had the book to promote and a tour had been arranged by the publishers before the official launch, on 9 October. How she even got to October I'll never know, to be honest.

But, despite the pain she was in, she took the view 'look ill, feel ill', and insisted on getting all glammed up to trek to Manchester on 7 October for *BBC Breakfast* – the first of the scheduled interviews.

Had anybody looked closely at the smiling pictures of her all over the front pages of the newspapers the next day, though, they might have noticed that I was permanently at her side, very firmly holding her arm. Sadly, it wasn't just to look like a loving husband for the cameras. She desperately needed the physical support.

Despite all her physical pain, it was such a relief for her to have everything out in the open. Lynda was always the first to admit she's not naturally the secretive type where emotions are involved, being more likely to wear her heart on her sleeve.

'I never deliberately deceived people. I just wasn't ready to tell the whole truth and face the inevitable media questioning,' she explained. Over and over again. Nor did she write about her illness for sympathy or for people to think she was any braver or any different to all the millions of cancer sufferers out there. Nevertheless, the tidal wave of love and support she received did her actress's ego – never high at the best of times – a world of good.

'Normally it's only after you're gone that people say such nice things about you and nobody's ever here to read their own obituary!' she'd laugh. And at times it did feel a bit as if she was attending her own enormous public wake.

In fact she was only half joking when she admitted that she'd started to worry in case she went on for months and it all got embarrassing. If so, she'd even chosen the title for a follow up book – *Hang on! There's Something I Forgot to Mention . . .!*

I think the embarrassment of her surviving by some miracle would have been the very last of her worries. And mine.

*

What we didn't know at the time was that Lynda's former colleague on the *Loose Women* panel, Carol McGiffin, was also battling cancer, but breast cancer not bowel cancer like Lynda. Carol had been diagnosed with a tumour in April, after finding a lump on holiday in Malaysia. But she hadn't told Lynda until she visited her with some of the other *Loose Women* at home.

As she later explained, 'I thought it would be really unfair of me to tell Lynda about my situation. She was such an unselfish person, so she would have loved it if there was someone else to worry about.'

Correct, Carol. You obviously knew her well. Carol came clean, though, when she and some of the other panellists turned up in a minibus for afternoon tea and champagne at our house. Even when she could no longer make sandwiches and bake cakes herself, Lynda liked to entertain her guests properly and had called in Maison Blanc to do the catering. Champagne was on tap to break the ice and ease any awkward moments, and Lynda joked that she'd just have to settle for an extra swig of morphine herself!

Her reaction to poor Carol's news was typically blunt. 'Fucking hell! Not you an' all!' And of course they all burst out laughing and were their usual loud selves. After a while, though, Lynda was looking tired and I had to tell them what a brilliant actress she was but that, underneath that act, she was exhausted. It was time for them to leave with their signed copies of her new book hot off the press. In fact very few people received signed copies because the end came before she got round to doing a proper signing.

They were all perfectly understanding – Carol, Jane McDonald, Denise Welch, Kate Thornton and Lisa Maxwell. I followed them out to the car park to say good-bye properly and explain that things really were not looking good. There were plenty of tears and hugs all round so we were there ages.

Lynda's last TV interview was a recorded one for *Loose Women* when she was on the show with Janet Street-Porter and Coleen Nolan. More than 2 million viewers – twice as many as normal, apparently – tuned in to watch Lynda tell how she wanted to be remembered as an honest person and explain her plan to stop her chemo. Somehow she still managed to look glam, but underneath that loose pink linen top she was skin and bone. That once lovely soft, sexy body ruined by cancer. Fuck You, Cancer.

I was sitting, watching tearfully in the studio audience as she put everyone at ease by cracking jokes about her situation. 'As you know, I wanted to win an Oscar at seventy-five for best newcomer. Sadly that's gone out of the window!'

Still she insisted that she was determined to make it to

Christmas. 'Bloody right I am. I AM!' she told them. If only it was that simple, my lover. I say my lover, but we hadn't been lovers for months and months now. We'd gone from making love every day to celibacy almost overnight, even before the operation. Lynda wrote in her book that she missed the physical side of our relationship and so did I, but it just became impossible between chemo, hospital, general sickness and lack of energy. The last thing I wanted was for her to be worrying about my needs. We all have to make sacrifices and while our sex life had always been so important to both of us, our love was way stronger than just sex. Way, way stronger.

When Coleen started welling up on air, Lynda even comforted her by saying: 'Don't cry, it's going to be fine.' Nevertheless your own mask did start to slip a bit, B, when everyone stood up and gave you your very last standing ovation. I could tell you were getting choked.

Of course neither of us really knew whether it would be fine or not. Lynda hadn't wanted any sort of dramatic deathbed scene; she just wanted to slip away quietly and peacefully, already out of it on drugs. You can't help but think about the end coming, and you do keep asking yourself, what will you do when the final thing happens? Maybe some people would call me callous, but it was just a fact of life. I knew the day was going to come. What would I do?

*

A week after Lynda's *Loose Women* appearance, I was to find out. But for the next few days at least I had to stay positive and keep a lid on all my own feelings and fears. It wasn't too hard, though, because I honestly thought she might still make it. But it was all so quick and sudden at the end.

On Friday, 10 October, I'd taken her in for chemo as normal and brought her home. I knew in my heart of hearts she was in a lot of pain, though she was trying not to show it, and I knew that she should be staying in hospital.

By one the next morning, I was woken up by her saying I'd have to take her in because she was in horrific pain. I later discovered it was the secondaries in the liver pushing up her rib cage. Little bastards.

Fortunately, they managed to get the pain under control and she was quite chirpy. I stayed with her all week, 24/7, sleeping on a camp bed right beside her. She never wanted the nurses to take her to the loo; she wanted me to lift her on and off the commode. I still had my uses!

All Lynda really wanted was to die at home and everything was in hand to bring her back on Friday, 17 October. Thanks to the North London Hospice, Barnet Council and the Macmillan cancer nurses, a hospital bed, chair and commode were delivered on the Thursday and all the necessary palliative care system was in place. When Lynda was sleeping, I'd quickly slipped out to John Lewis to buy a new single duvet, pillows and three sets of their best white Egyptian cotton bedlinen for her at home. Nothing but the best. I'd been on the internet earlier that week to buy the best looking and comfiest wheelchair I could find to take her home in. Thank God for the Range Rover and its electric steps. It made it so much easier to physically get her in and out of the passenger seat. It was a job we'd got off to a fine art. Working together right up to the end.

'If you think I am going in a wheelchair, it ain't happening!' she warned me, as proud as ever. She never wanted the press to get hold of a picture of her in a wheelchair.

'I hate to tell you this, Babe, but you are,' I replied, just as adamant about it as she was. For this once I had to ignore her wishes completely as by now she'd deteriorated so rapidly that she could no longer walk more than a few steps. Whatever else she wanted to believe.

She was getting ready to come home on the Friday but suddenly terrible pains came back over her. At worst, it was 'like giving birth to an elephant', she used to say. Obviously, I've never given birth, but perhaps women reading this might understand how bad it was from her description.

I knew then, for certain, that she wouldn't make it to Christmas. She knew herself that it was the end of the end, even though we never said it in as many words.

The doctor said she'd have to stay in because the pain wasn't under enough control. At home I couldn't legally give her the painkilling injection she needed, although I would have done and taken the rap for it afterwards if she'd been in agony and I'd had it to hand. No question. I've been to prison once; I could do it again if it meant sparing her pain.

But it was up to the doctors to decide that there was no guarantee that a specially trained, legally allowed nurse would get to us quickly enough in traffic to deliver the jab and spare her agony. I suppose I knew that it was the right decision, even though now I regret that Lynda never got her wish to end her days here. But had she come home, I knew I'd have ended up dialling 999 and she'd have been heading straight back in to hospital by ambulance.

She slept all Friday and, when Saturday arrived, she was still really tired. She'd stopped eating and drinking. I just sat and watched her sleeping. I knew things weren't right. By 3 p.m. I just knew, I just knew. It was time to accept the inevitable. There was nothing there any more; no quality of life, nothing . . .

The telly in her room was permanently switched off now and it was quiet and peaceful. I'd taken hundreds of cards in for her to read and I sat there looking through them all as she lay there. Around 11.30 p.m. I decided to slip out, leaving her still sleeping, to walk over to a little church on Marylebone Road to pray for her. The doors were closed so I just sat down on the stone steps outside and prayed and prayed for Him to save her. And cried and cried and cried. Don't even ask me how long for because I haven't a clue. We'd both taken comfort in prayer. Even though Lynda admitted to being a fair-weather Christian, who turned up to church for the big occasions like Christmas and Easter, she had a strong faith. Although it had been tested big time by cancer and she didn't expect a man with a beard to meet her at the pearly gates, she believed in a God and believed that He had helped her cope with all this. She had prayed throughout for me and the boys.

'I still trust He will come up with something lovely for them all when I'm no longer here, even if it's only that they find acceptance and get on with their lives,' she told friends.

I still find myself praying a fair bit now. Whenever I am in a new town or city, I like to go into the local church or cathedral and just sit there; maybe light a candle for Lynda and ask the Good Lord to take care of her. I enjoy the peace and it makes me feel close to her.

At 11 a.m. on the day she died, she was so poorly that I was back in church saying this time to God, 'You've got to take her.' I didn't want her to suffer any more now. It was time to let go; it really wasn't about me now.

*

I'd woken up early and I knew as soon as I saw Lynda that things had changed. For the last week she'd been waking at 2 a.m. and 6 a.m. because of the pain, but that last night she'd slept right through. I gave her a kiss and sat there in silence, holding her hand and re-reading all the cards again and again.

I was also trying to keep her mouth moist with a sponge on a stick, and she half woke up so I tried to get her to drink. Her skinny legs had started to swell up, which I knew wasn't a good sign. She fell back asleep and I slipped out for a quiet word with the Good Lord. I took Holy Communion and begged him to end her suffering.

When I left the church I popped into the wine bar next door and sank a large glass of wine to steady me before going back into the London Clinic. On the way there, I got a text from Chris, the lovely, caring regular pain relief nurse, to say she was coming in at 1 p.m. I wasn't expecting her, but I knew why and what was coming.

When she arrived, she nodded at me to pop outside Lynda's room for a chat, and she told me then that Lynda had got forty-eight hours. Tops.

'I don't even think she's got that. I think she's going to go today,' I replied.

'Well, we don't know . . .' she added, but I don't remember her disputing it.

I started to phone a few people and the boys came

straight in. I left Michael and Robbie alone with her to say their private goodbyes to their mum. Bradley, Jean and her daughter Martha, Peter Delaney, his friend Paul and Nickolas Grace all seemed to arrive together. Against her nature, this was the one time Lynda didn't want a dramatic goodbye scene, a 'to-do' as she put it. No black lace or too many tears.

As it was, she never woke up again, so in a sense she got her wish to just slip away. Hearing is the last sense to go, so I carried on talking to her all the time. As I slipped her gold and diamond wedding ring off her finger and onto mine (where it still sits, rubbing next to my own wedding ring today), I told her I loved her. I don't know how many times I said it.

My belief – and I have no doubt about it – is that some-one comes and takes the soul of the dying person. I was at one side holding her and Nickolas Grace was at the other when it happened. Suddenly she looked up as if she was staring into a light and she smiled. It was exactly 7.50 p.m. and I kissed her, told her I loved her again and again and again, and she left. The Good Lord had taken her out of my arms. It was peaceful and she was not in any pain; obvi-ously the drugs had kicked in.

You know instantly when the soul has gone. The body

of my wife was left lying there, but her soul had gone from the room. Lynda Bellingham had left the building.

I don't want to sound like a fruitcake, but I'd like to think that her spirit returned two weeks later in the form of a white butterfly at her funeral in St Bartholomew's, Crewkerne . . .

Outside in the corridor, the ward sister and nurses were all so kind. The day staff who should have finished at 8 p.m. wanted to stay on past their shift end to prepare Lynda, rather than letting the night nurses take over. I was touched by that and I know Lynda would have been. She liked them a lot.

Around 9.30 p.m. they'd done their job and I went back in to sit with Lynda alone for another hour or so, just talking to her, telling her how much I loved and would miss her. Then I took our clothes, her handbag, the cards and kissed her goodbye. Leaving without her, I cried non-stop all the way home.

We delayed the funeral in the hope that Sue Latimer could get back from Los Angeles to attend, but in the end she couldn't make it. There'd been plenty to do in the meantime, including taking back all the equipment that was never needed. You got your own way and never had to use that brand new wheelchair after all, didn't you, B? I donated it to North London Hospice – I hope someone who needed it got the benefit of it.

I threw myself into organizing the funeral. There was plenty to do – informing everybody, choosing hymns, buying flowers, organizing the wake, shopping for smart black suits for me and Lynda's son Michael. One of the worst jobs was registering Lynda's death the day after she died. I'd popped in to see her again and hand her over to Clive to take back to Crewkerne. One journey where you couldn't argue with the driver about which was the best route to take, B! A first, and last. Then I went to see the registrar, who I remember asking me to check that all the details on the certificate were correct. I saw it written in black ink: 'Mr Michael Pattemore, Widower', and the tears started again. Was that really who I was now? I hated that word 'widower'. It was so final.

One of the proudest moments of that week had to be when Prince Charles, no less, paid tribute to Lynda. He described her as a 'marvellous actress' and said he was 'greatly saddened' by news of her death as well as praising her 'tireless work' for other people. What about that, B? I cannot tell you how thrilled Lynda would have been by such an accolade. Who wouldn't?

Eventually the day of the big send-off arrived, and after a few wines too many the night before, I found myself lying alone in bed at Haselbury Mill, just outside Crewkerne.

I hadn't slept a wink and it was 6.30 a.m. By now, Lynda's grave should have been dug. The job had been left until the morning of the funeral so that the press couldn't get pictures of it. The local television station BBC West had already sent a film crew down there a few days beforehand.

When I originally bought the plots after my father died, I'd chosen the ones that were facing due east so they would catch the sun all day. I like to think that he and Lynda are lying in the sunshine. She always did like to sunbathe.

There'd been no sunshine the last time I'd been there, though, checking things out the week beforehand, because it was the day the clocks went back to mark the official end of British Summer Time. It was only tea time, but it was pitch black. We had to use torches to check with health and safety officials that my plans for a final surprise could go ahead . . .

In bed, desperate not to think about the day to come, I started reliving the first time I met Lynda in sunny Spain. By sheer coincidence it was exactly ten years ago to the day: 3 November 2004. Bizarre really. The funeral wasn't planned this day because of that. I reminded myself, also, of the really good news that Lynda's book (which later sold half a million copies) had shot to number one in the best-seller list. She'd have been so pleased and proud about that. As we all were.

I tried really hard to stay strong in front of the boys. I still do. I keep reminding myself and them that she's not suffering any more. We have to take comfort from that, and the fact that she slipped away so peacefully. Even now, when I am alone, I still cry about the unfairness of it all. It was no different early that morning. I tried to get up but just slumped straight back down on the corner of the bed, put my head in my hands and wept buckets.

Eventually I pulled myself together, had a shower, shaved, put on a clean shirt and checked on the boys in their room. After seeing they were hungover but otherwise okay, I headed downstairs for breakfast.

Our friend Peter Delaney was conducting Lynda's funeral service at noon and was waiting for me, along with my wonderful foster sisters and their family and various friends. Unable to stomach a thing, I gulped down an orange juice and took a cab to St Bartholomew's on the west side of Crewkerne with the ushers, John Chandler, Steve Markbride, Kevin Morfitt and Nickolas Grace. We needed to be there at 9 a.m. to meet up with a local deejay I'd hired to set up a sound system in church for Lynda's own final surprise song. Today had to be perfect for her. Absolutely perfect.

The press had beaten us there and were already waiting outside the ancient stone building. As soon as we arrived, the camera flashes started as we headed in to check with Clive, the funeral director, that everything was ready and in order.

Then I headed off alone to see Lynda one last time before the lid went on the solid mahogany coffin with the carving of The Last Supper on the side. Five years ago she'd seen one like it in the window of a funeral directors when she was on tour with *Calendar Girls*. There and then, she decided that was what we should both be buried in. Little did she know she would be lying in it so soon dressed in her best clothes. By the way, I finally found the shoes in a special cloth bag, not in the Ikea rack I built her in her dressing room with all the other pairs of shoes. In the end, though, Clive couldn't slip them on as the shape of her feet had changed.

Even seeing her there, it didn't register that my gorgeous wife had gone. I'd visited her there the night before because I'd wanted to check the coffin over. It was the first time I'd seen it. I'd explained to Clive what I wanted on the day he collected Lynda from hospital and he'd told me that he didn't have one in stock but would get hold of one. Later, he'd shown me pictures of three or four on the internet and I'd chosen the one I thought Lynda would want. I wasn't disappointed, it was perfect.

For the second time, the tears came flooding out of me as saw her lying there looking so beautiful and peaceful. I held her hands and told her I loved her. Over and over again, kissing her on the lips, hands and forehead. 'We will meet again, my lover,' I whispered. And I believed it; I still do.

To the best of my knowledge, I'd carried out all her last wishes. She wanted to be buried in the navy blue dress she wore to receive her OBE in at Buckingham Palace in March.

Back at the hotel, I changed into a black shirt and suit, putting a red hankie in my breast pocket, and headed off for my mum's house with Michael, Robbie, Brad, Jean, her daughter Martha, and Lynda's old friend Pat Hay. My daughter Stacey joined us there, where my stepbrother Michael handed out glasses of wine.

I must have had two or three to calm me by the time the hearse arrived carrying Lynda's coffin. On top was one huge spray of white and green flowers – all her favourites but mainly roses. Jean had bought those. I'd had some made up into wreaths spelling Lynda and Mum, and organized displays for the church. They must have cost a good two grand, maybe more, which some people might think extravagant. But Lynda loved her flowers, and it was important for me and Jean that she got the best today. It was the last thing we could do for her. So why not?

In the car behind the hearse, my mind raced with memories of all the good times we'd had together. We crawled through the streets lined with ordinary people paying their respects, and it was the same when we arrived at the church. People had turned out in their hundreds to say goodbye. That was so nice. Lynda always had time for her fans.

It was my idea that the boys and me would carry Lynda's coffin in and out of the packed church. It wasn't anything we'd done before and it was really heavy. But with me and Michael at the front, Robbie and Brad in the middle, and two of Clive's men at the back, we managed to hoist her onto our shoulders and carry her down the aisle as the organist played Elgar's 'Nimrod', from the 'Enigma Variations'. Lynda loved that.

I was crying and so was everyone around me. I don't know how I did it as I didn't feel anything, but somehow I cut my ear on the side of the coffin and by the time we reached the altar it was really bleeding. As I sat down in my pew, people started shoving tissues in my hand, and I was grateful my shirt was black.

The service began and I just stared at the coffin as, around me, everyone started singing 'Lead Us, Heavenly Father, Lead Us'. Lynda had never got round to choosing the hymns for the service so, with Peter Delaney's help, we went for the ones we had at our wedding and arranged for the choir to sing Lynda's favourite carol, 'Away in a Manger'. There were plenty of tears for that one as Peter explained it was to mark her love of Christmas and her great wish to be with us for one last one.

Lisa Maxwell, Lynda's old colleague from *The Bill* and *Loose Women* did the first reading from the epistle to the Romans, 8:31–9, then Gyles Brandreth led the tributes.

Sometimes sadness and celebration can go hand in hand. Here we are in this beautiful, amazing church in Michael's home town, saying goodbye to lovely Lynda. Brave, beautiful, brilliant, funny, fabulous Lynda. As we say goodbye to her in here, her book is a number one bestseller. I think she would have liked to have gone out on a high.

I first met her nearly forty years ago when we were introduced by Biggins. Of course, I fell for her at once. She was so funny and so sexy – even gay men fancied her.

Shakespeare has one of his leading ladies remind us that all things must die, passing through nature to eternity.

Lynda was an extraordinary force of nature, intelligent, gifted, generous, funny, feisty, open, honest, kind and caring.

I don't think I have known anyone more alive than

Lynda Bellingham. She showed us how to live and in the last year or two of her life she taught us how to die – with grace, courage, humour and acceptance.

She rang me three weeks ago and said she was in a good place. 'I am sad for the boys and Michael but I'm all right.' She was all right, she was the best and she was our friend. Aren't we the lucky ones?

Without a shadow of a doubt, Gyles, we were. Jean followed him at the lectern to pay tribute to her sister and was followed by a taped tribute from Lynda La Plante, who was unable to fly over from Los Angeles.

Maureen Lipman, who'd been at drama school with Lynda, was next and recalled Lynda's 'sudden honking laughter' and her 'beautiful brown eyes'.

After everybody sang 'Love Divine, All Loves Excelling', Jane McDonald gave her tribute.

Like Lynda La Plante, Lynda's long-time agent, Sue Latimer, gave a taped tribute from Los Angeles. Carol McGiffin was down on the printed order of service to follow her but she was suffering from the effects of her latest chemo and was too ill to be there. Lynda, of all people, would have understood that. Christopher Timothy told of Lynda's acting skills and generosity. Nickolas Grace spoke about how they first met in 1966 and their friendship through the years.

The choir sang 'God Be in My Head' by Walford Davies, then Denise Welch was next, and under orders from Lynda not to stand on ceremony but to share her bawdy humour. Good old Denise – or Densie as her friends know her – she made everyone laugh. After telling one of Lynda's favourite jokes about two little old ladies sitting on a park bench, she read a funny poem she'd written herself. It read:

I'll miss you Lynda very much as will everybody
> here,
There is no need to say how much you are loved,
> as today that is abundantly clear.
If you are looking down from wherever you are
> I am sure you will be having a hoot,
at the odd bods that loved you so dearly,
> like Biggins in that bloody pink suit!

'Your humour is what I will remember and the dirtiest laugh known to man,' she went on.

It was Biggins's task, in that very bright suit, to end the eulogies from the showbiz world. He had everyone laughing and crying when he turned to the coffin and said: 'Lynda ... Bellie ... we will cry, but eventually at the end of the day we all love you. We will always love you as you were so, so special.'

'Wouldn't she have loved today?' he asked. I still like to think she actually was there, because of what happened after the choir sang 'Lord Make Me an Instrument of Your Peace' and Sue Holderness read William Shakespeare's Sonnet 116.

As Michael and Robbie stood at the front of the church, reading a loving letter their mum had written for them, the sun suddenly shone through the high Tudor style windows. Out of nowhere, a white butterfly flew off one of the golden stone sills and began fluttering all around above us at the top of the church.

If you believe in these things, a butterfly is a common sign that the spirit of the person who has just died is still around. A comforting symbol of love, like a white feather.

When I took the lectern, I spoke about my first meeting with the 'Oxo lady' a decade ago. Happy days. I thanked her wonderful friends, who were understandably protective of her, for accepting me and told them how meeting Biggins was like meeting the in-laws!

'But you have all been *fantastic* and thank you for accepting me. A few of you – and you know who you are – have become really close and I love you dearly.

'Over the last ten years, I've seen the love and respect that Lynda gives to all her friends and her fans on the street – it's what makes her so special.

'She had more stamina and energy than anyone I've

ever met. Nothing was too much trouble. She was always there – to help as much as she can. Whether it was a friend in distress or one of her many charity commitments.'

I repeated some of my wedding speech, when I'd reassured them all that she was safe with me and, even though I may not look like a knight in shining armour, I would always protect her.

And I did try to keep my promise to keep her safe, I carried on. 'I'm a practical man and I think I can fix most things. But the only thing I couldn't do was protect her from this vicious cancer. That was so hard and it made me feel so helpless. In my wildest dreams, I could not have imagined finding this warm and wonderful woman. I have never in my life got on with someone as well as Lynda – my soulmate. The most gorgeous, giving, loving lady in the world. I was Mr Truly Lucky.

'Thank you, Lynda, for letting me be the lucky, lucky man who shared your life for ten wonderful years. This last year has taught me a lot about love, marriage, true friendship – and most of all, a lot about Lynda. I always knew she was wonderful but now I know she was brave beyond belief – and always, always, trying to protect us all from distress, even when she was so ill.'

Of course I had to give the last word to Lynda so I read her poem out that she'd written for me in *There's Something I've Been Dying to Tell You*:

To Michael

Remember:
That morning in Spain
The full English going down a storm
'You want a mortgage?
Not a problem, Miss B.'
Already an intimacy
A connection with a like soul
Watching me in your car mirror, your flash
        hairdresser's car!
Sussing me out, weighing me up.

Remember:
A day of laughter and sunshine,
And way too much wine,
Then goodbye and thanks and back to London
        for me,
You returned to the bar for another glass of Riscali.
Then texts and phone calls,
An invitation from me,
To dinner, anytime.
'Your daughter is with you?'
Oh damn ... How lovely!
'Bring her as well
Not a problem at all.'

Remember:
Instant contact, electricity and passion
Certainly lust and possibly need?
Reaching out for affection, while grappling to find
That still small voice that says
What?
Ah, now we have it.
A sentence so simple
So hard to define
To learn to trust once again
To step over that line.

Remember:
Then came death to our beginnings
Losing my parents in one month
I quickly found you
The centre, the nub of it all
My rock, my knight, my lover.
You made me wake up and grab the life
That was offered, so real and so different
From the sham I was living.
So alone and so lonely
Just me and my boys.
Thank God for my boys.
Could you breach that wall of motherly love?
Not easily, but you did.

Remember:
Truth and lies?
People trying to crush us with their cynical
    mediocrity
Their sad distorted negativity.
'Not a problem,' you'd say
'Not a problem at all.'
You can do anything
Heal a wound or burst a boil
Life does not scare you
Not anything at all.
But death does, doesn't it, my lover?
Death is unfair and cruel
Not in your remit at all.

Remember:
How we talked of our life together
When all our chores had been done
Twenty years, fifteen at least
To open our box of ten years together.
Yes, short but oh so sweet.
Don't give up now, my lover
Do some of the things we promised we would do
Please guard the door and the lid to our trinkets
Our box of 'remembers'.

Remember:
You always aim for the best
We have had it and you will keep alive, though
    I'm dead.
It's only a word so say it, spit it out
Toss it away in the wind
Think only of good things and now this is it
I have come to the point, round and round I go
They are almost unspeakable
So precious have they grown
As always I tell you
In my own way
I love you, Michael Pattemore
There's nothing more I can say.

As I ended, I turned to the coffin and said: 'I love you Lynda. Until we meet again . . .' And the butterfly flew off as suddenly as it had arrived. God bless you, my Lynda.

Afterwards we all sang the Women's Institute anthem, 'Jerusalem'. Even before Lynda's connection with *Calendar Girls*, she'd always loved that hymn and it had been sung at our wedding. As the service ended, there wasn't a dry eye in the congregation of 350, but determined everyone should leave on a high, Lynda arranged for one last laugh.

*

As we carried her coffin back down the aisle and out of church, Ethel Merman's voice singing 'There's No Business Like Show Business' from the musical *Annie Get Your Gun* came booming out. The stunt worked perfectly and everyone went out laughing. Even I had to smile through my tears.

At the graveside across town at Townsend Cemetery, I had my own surprise lined up that even Lynda hadn't known I was planning. As she was being lowered into the ground and her closest family and friends had thrown white roses onto the coffin, there was a spectacular flash.

Determined that my wonderful wife would go out with a bang, I'd arranged for a two-minute firework display. Six grand's worth but, really, what was money any more? It just didn't have the same value. It had no value. Still doesn't. As everybody clapped and cheered, I knew I'd done the right thing. Lynda – who I know was looking down and watching – would have been amazed.

Back at a reception at Haselbury Mill, ITV executive and Lynda's former *Loose Women* boss, Sue Walton, had put together an emotional slide show of some of her film clips.

Once more, Lynda cheered everyone up at the end of it. In her famous jolly fashion, just before the credits of the last show rolled, her old voice rang out across the wake: 'Sadly, time to go!' It was, B, and you bloody well went, didn't you? But I also know you didn't really. Your spirit is still very much alive. And still all around me.

CHAPTER 11

HELLO AGAIN?

......

It is less than a month since I lost my wonderful wife and I am at home waiting for an official ITV car to arrive and take me to the *Loose Women* studios to talk about her live on air.

Suddenly my mobile rings and a woman with a softly spoken voice is at the other end of the line. She explains that she's the psychic medium, Yvonne Williams, in Crewkerne, who is returning my call from a few days ago.

'Lynda is with me,' she tells me and, to be honest, I don't believe it. But because I am desperate to, and because she's been so highly recommended by a couple of friends down there, I let Yvonne carry on.

She says a couple of things I can't remember now, before telling me a couple of things that stop me dead in my tracks. Completely.

'Lynda's saying she's glad you finally found the shoes. It's a pity they didn't fit.'

Now that is scary. I only spoke to one journalist the morning after Lynda died – someone from *Yours* magazine – and I remember telling her that I hadn't been able to find the shoes I wanted her to be buried in. I think the information was then picked up by the nationals. But apart from Clive the undertaker, nobody other than that *Yours* journalist knew that when I eventually found them, days later, they no longer fitted Lynda because her body had changed. She hadn't used that information out of respect because it was so personal at such a sensitive time. So how the hell does this medium know?

The second thing Yvonne throws me with is when she says that Lynda is sitting with her dog, the black and white one that is in the photo on top of the television in our bedroom.

Star! She had to be talking about Star, who was the family pet Lynda bought for Michael when he was a little boy. He was a black-and-white sheepdog that had come from a litter born on the farm when Lynda was filming *All Creatures Great and Small*. He was called Star because he had a white star on the top of his head. Now Lynda did write about Star in her first autobiography, *Lost and Found*, so that information was out there in the public and Yvonne could easily have read it. But how the hell did she know about the photo and where it was? Even I couldn't say for certain as we have so many framed personal photos in our apartment. Everything from Lynda with the Queen or some well-known face to family pictures, holiday pictures and wedding pictures are all over the walls, shelves and tables in every room. Dozens and dozens of them.

By this time, my car had arrived and I had to go, so I hung up after making an appointment to meet Yvonne face to face and went on my way, thinking: *Wow!* My scepticism was disappearing.

When I arrived back after doing *Loose Women* that afternoon, the first thing I did was go into our bedroom and check out the pictures on the shelf on top of our TV. Sitting right there was a colour photograph of Lynda and Star. Bizarre.

It's funny, but our bedroom is the place I feel closest to Lynda. It's also where I miss her the most. Every morning when I first wake up, always still on my own side, my arm reaches across the bed expecting to find her there. Every night, the last thing I do is kiss my fingers – including the little one on my left hand where her wedding ring sits, and touch her pillow with them. It's become my way of saying 'goodnight, darling' to her. When you've been with someone you love so much, you just cannot believe they are gone. You simply cannot get your head round it.

Day after day after day, you wake up and you think they are going to be there and everything is going to be okay again. But they never are and it never is. Nor are they ever going to be. I'd give anything to have her back.

A couple of really odd things have happened in there as well.

One weekday morning I woke up a bit earlier than my normal time of 7 a.m. and, for some reason, I just lay there pretty much in la-la land. Usually I get up straight away, but suddenly Lynda was there again, just lying beside me. But it wasn't the Lynda with the white hair and cancer as I'd seen her last. It was the old, sexy Lynda with dark hair and brown eyes. The bird I fell in love with. I don't know how to explain it; it was just surreal.

To be honest, I thought I had my lady back again. But only for a split second. I didn't even get as far as reaching out to touch her because the phone on the bedside table rang. It was Bradley, who was already out at work, ringing to tell me that somebody needed paying for one of his jobs and would be popping round to the apartment for his wedge in the next hour. As I came round, Lynda had vanished, disappeared. Just as quickly as she'd appeared. You might say I hadn't woken up properly and it was just a dream. I cannot describe it any better than I have because it all happened so quickly. All I can say is it didn't feel like a dream; it felt real somehow. And there was certainly no alcohol involved because it was early morning.

Another morning not so long ago, I walked back into our bedroom to clear up a few things and there was a strange smell. It just hit you. Whoa! It took me a while to realize what it was, and then it came to me that it was Lynda's perfume. She always wore the same one and it was very distinctive. Searching around the room, I found a bottle of Chanel Cristalle and recognized it straight away as the same one Lynda had always worn, which was now giving off a strong scent in our bedroom. Again, all very strange.

Both me and Lynda had always believed that our spirits would move on when we were no longer here. We'd always believed this. Where does that belief come from? Good question. And one I can't answer. You either believe or you don't. End of.

We both believed that if you were on this planet for X amount of years, that wasn't it. No way. We just couldn't see it. We've all got our own spirit inside us. That's what makes us all different. No, it is not the end. Definitely not. Just as I know Lynda is still around me, I know we will meet again. Funny, but I don't fear death at all now; not one little bit. I have got no qualms at all; I am not frightened at all. It sounds bizarre, but I know Lynda will be waiting for me. I know it isn't the end.

I wish in a way, though, He'd taken me instead. Lynda was just so full of life. It's hard, bloody hard being here on my own, and I am still taking it a day and a week at a time.

There have been moments, when I first lost her, when I won't deny that the idea of suicide crossed my mind, though not in any serious way that I'd do anything about. I couldn't inflict that on my family, I think too much about them all. Besides, I believe – despite not being a Catholic – that if you commit suicide you end up in purgatory which means I wouldn't be with Lynda anyway. And that ain't happening! When I do go, I want to know I am going to meet up with my soulmate again.

On the last Friday in November, coming up to six weeks since Lynda died, I drove down to Crewkerne for my first face-to-face appointment with Yvonne. I don't know what I was expecting, but she was a lovely, very ordinary lady who was working from an apartment in a building that used to be the old grammar school. It was close to the cemetery where Lynda and my dad are buried but that didn't feel at all spooky. In fact it was very spiritual.

I was trying to keep an open mind still but Yvonne caught me off guard when she said a few things about Lynda and my old dad who I miss like mad as well.

Unlike Lynda, my dad had been diagnosed with

prostate cancer only six weeks before he died. I'll never forget it. It was a beautiful Friday afternoon and me and Lynda were in Cambridge, eating ice cream on one of the bridges watching the punts go by. My phone went off and it was my dad, saying, 'Michael, I've got prostate cancer.'

'When's all this happened?' I asked.

'I've just found out.'

'I'll be down tomorrow morning,' I promised.

Lynda was appearing in *Calendar Girls* and had two shows to do, so I went down to Somerset first thing the next morning. My dad had kind of worked out himself that he had something wrong with him when he got back from a holiday at my villa in Spain and he couldn't carry the cases upstairs. He had to open them downstairs and take all the stuff up bit by bit.

I'm quite proud to say that I went to every single hospital appointment with him along with my stepbrother Michael. One day he was in for tests and a biopsy when the doctor came in to the waiting room where me and Michael were. I'll never forget him telling us, 'Your dad has got six weeks to live.'

He put his hand on my shoulder and said, 'I know exactly how you feel,' and I flipped and asked, 'How do you fucking know how I feel?'

He replied, 'My dad died of exactly the same thing,' and I felt terrible. After apologizing, we told him we didn't want my dad to be told, but about a week later Michael rang to tell me that the GP had told my dad how long he had left to live.

I went ballistic, phoned the GP surgery and demanded to speak to the doctor, who explained he had a duty of care. He'd known my dad for forty plus years and he had a right to know. I drove straight down to Crewkerne and gave Dad a big hug.

'You know, don't you?' he said.

'Yes, but I really didn't want you to know,' I replied.

Now I know the doctor was right; my dad had a right to know and it allowed him and us to sort a few things out. He had always wanted to be cremated, for instance, but I never wanted that for myself and I told him why. I just feel that when you are buried, there is something left of the person, there at the grave. Like now with Lynda . . .

Out of the blue, my dad said he'd been thinking about what I'd said and decided he wanted to be buried. He looked round at my stepmum and said to her, 'You're going to be buried as well, aren't you?' 'It looks like it!' came the reply. I went out and bought two double plots at Crewkerne Cemetery, one for them and one for me and Lynda. Me and my old mum, now eighty-nine, blind and in a home, will be next in there.

The following Saturday, I drove back down and spent all day sitting with my dad, asking him questions about his life. I am so glad now I did. As much as we think we know our parents, we don't know everything. There were loads of things I didn't realize, such as where he worked when he first left school. I had no idea. When I read the eulogy at St Bartholomew's I used it all. I started off by asking, who is this man, Joseph Frederick Pattemore? I must have been up there for twenty minutes, repeating the stories I'd only just heard myself and may never have known.

I am telling my dad's story because it is such a different experience of death to the one I had with Lynda. Perhaps you can see why, when we were told she could expect to have another two years after the colonoscopy, it sounded an eternity.

So what's best: to know or not to know when your loved one is dying? To be given hope and a bit of time like Lynda, or no hope and no time like my dad? Having been through both scenarios, I'd say without a shadow of a doubt that knowing, and being given hope and time are better.

We put Lynda's two years away in a box, and you can let yourself think that a lot can happen in two years. And the worst might not happen. It gives you time to tell the person how much you love them and is a reminder not to say anything you might later regret. With my dad there was no hope. There was nothing they could do; they made that quite clear. That's harder to deal with.

I met a lovely Irish lady on a trip to Dublin who lost her husband very suddenly after an accident on a building site. He went out to work one morning and never came back to her. No goodbye or anything. There was no doubt in her mind and mine that it is better to know that your husband or wife is dying and to be able to say all the things you want to say to them first.

Yvonne the medium is helping me cope with my bereavement. I've been seeing her every month and the stuff she comes out with, including some very personal things I don't want to go into here ... it is quite amazing really and very comforting.

But there was one thing she said on either the first or second meeting that I am still not so sure about. She drew the initials in the air of a lady she says I will 'end up with'.

Immediately I laughed and said, 'No!' Now don't get me wrong, I know I might not feel this way forever, but at the moment I am not interested in 'ending up' with anybody else. And I cannot imagine for one minute that I will ever get married again, despite what Lynda said I should do.

It is interesting though that the woman she mentioned,

someone who is in the public eye as Lynda was, was someone Lynda had once asked me if I fancied. I completely rubbished the idea. 'Why would I want anyone else when I have you, Babes?' I asked her. And I meant it. But I did add jokingly, 'But if I wasn't with you I'd probably be after her. Like a rat up a drainpipe!' She saw the funny side because she knew I would never cheat on her. Ever. It just seems a real coincidence that Yvonne came up with the initials of that same woman . . .

Now I know Lynda genuinely wanted me to meet someone else and I also know that I like the company of women. I have taken a couple of ladies out for dinner. Just friends. But I have absolutely no interest in replacing Lynda. When you've had something so good like we had, you do take it for granted and think everybody has the same thing and they don't. Lynda will never, ever be replaced. That's for certain.

I was talking to Bradley about relationships and the future recently and how I really don't need another relationship. It is lonely, but you somehow do get used to it. Well, you do and you don't. The only thing is you've got to keep yourself busy. You've really got to keep busy. And I have. Still do.

Around the same time as my first visit to Yvonne, Lynda also managed to communicate with me from beyond the grave in a rather more conventional way. I made an appointment to see my local GP to ask for sleeping pills because I couldn't get a decent night's sleep.

He told me that he was going to ring me that day anyway because Lynda had asked him to. Apparently she'd been in to see him in her last weeks without telling me. I'm still trying to work out how she managed it without me knowing because I didn't let her out of my sight! She'd told him she was worried about me going off the rails when she'd gone and she'd made him promise to haul me in after a month and look after me.

The morning after she died I told people that the Good Lord had taken her and she was probably looking down on us now. Either that or organizing everyone up there. Well, I hadn't banked on her still organizing us down here as well! I ask you!

The doctor quizzed me about how much I was drinking and I answered flippantly, 'Too much.' Admitting to two or three bottles a day, he said he was going to sort that out and prescribed me a course of pills that would completely take away the urge for alcohol.

I agreed and started taking them as he'd told me. Two, three times a day on the first day; two, morning, midday and teatime and three at night on the second; two, morning and evening on the third; then one morning and one at night afterwards. He'd warned me not to drink as I would be very sick.

I didn't and happily they worked. As well as taking the urge to drink away completely, they helped me sleep right through the night. Amazing. Physically, I felt tons better and even started going to the gym with Bradley.

The next time I saw Yvonne, she said that Lynda was really proud of me for locking the bottles away. How could she have known? I didn't tell her anything on my visits; I always kept completely schtum because I was determined not to give anything away. Bizarre. I always go straight to Lynda's grave and have a good cry after seeing Yvonne.

Perhaps Christmas wasn't the best of times to be on the wagon, though. Any Christmas is hard when people everywhere drink more than normal. But we were all dreading Christmas 2014 because it should have been our last one with Lynda. She wanted more than anything to be here with us and of course she wasn't.

Every day in the run up, I spent a lot of time crying, particularly when I was reading and re-reading all the condolence and Christmas cards with special messages that were flooding in. We literally got hundreds and hundreds. The other thing keeping me busy was the fundraising, and I am proud to say that an appeal set up in Lynda's name has to date raised more than £150,000 for Justin Stebbing's charity Action Against Cancer. We'd had a plate at the back of the church at the funeral where people could donate in lieu of flowers and the donations had kept on coming. Again, Lynda would be overwhelmed and so proud. All she wanted was to help others, but she would never have dreamt she'd have achieved as much as she actually did.

As Christmas was approaching, it became more and more obvious that I couldn't be at home without Lynda. I just couldn't face it. I was keeping myself busy in the run up to it, organizing the Fortnum and Mason champagne and chocolate boxes and the Christmas cards to send to people on the list on the computer – all 300 of them. Lynda's novel, *The Boy I Love*, had come out weeks beforehand and I'd done a few interviews about it, including appearing on Lorraine Kelly's show. That was really hard, being back in a television studio on the South Bank again without Lynda. For a *Yours* magazine interview, I'd done a shoot with the family and the photographer had sent us a photograph which he'd agreed we could use for our personally printed Christmas cards. We were all on it: Stacey, Brad, Michael, Robbie, my grandsons Cooper and Oakley, and me. Lynda would've liked that, even though we all looked jollier than we really felt at the time.

News was also filtering through that the Oxo Christmas advert from 1984 would be screened during *Coronation Street* on Christmas Day in memory of Lynda, and that everybody involved in the initiative would give their time for free. A donation would be made by Premier Foods to Action Against Cancer. In the advert, Lynda the Oxo mum is preparing Christmas dinner and drinking sherry as all the family show her their presents.

It finishes with the line from the daughter: 'Everyone had the most wonderful Christmas ever. And Mummy? Mummy made the gravy.'

Emotional stuff, because one thing was for sure, her real family wasn't expecting the most wonderful Christmas ever. And none of Mummy's delicious gravy either. As sure as hell.

After a lot of thought I decided to escape altogether and go to Dubai with Brad from 22 December to 2 January, when Christmas and New Year were well and truly over. Michael and Robbie were planning to spend some of the day with their father, and it just wasn't going to work staying here. Dubai also had special memories because it was where Lynda had taken me for my fiftieth birthday. Good times.

But, to be honest, there was no such thing as the right thing to do. Whatever I did, wherever I was, I knew I was still going to miss her like mad.

In mid-December I found myself back at the doctor's having a tear duct on my left eye checked out. I was told that there was a problem with a granuloma so my nose was anaesthetized and the lump was cut off and sent for analysis.

The first question I asked was, 'Is it the Big C?'

'Not at all,' came the reply. There's nothing like seeing someone go through terminal cancer to make you so shit scared of it.

Just before I left for Dubai I'd arranged to go to Wolverhampton to see Ben Stock in the panto, *Cinderella*, at the Grand Theatre there. Ben had been in panto the previous year with Lynda and we both liked him. It was probably not the greatest idea in the world, though, as I couldn't stop crying. It brought back so many memories. Lynda should have been up there on stage with him.

One of the last places I went before flying out to Dubai was Lynda's grave, where I'd arranged for Christmas wreaths to be laid for her and my dad. It shouldn't be like this . . .

We arrived in Dubai on Christmas Eve and that same day we hung some Oxo cubes for baubles on the Christmas tree in the hotel reception. I'd packed a box specially in my case and people probably thought I was mad. The least of my troubles right then.

On Christmas Day I woke up around 7 a.m. and my first thought was Lynda and all the good times. Even I used to get a stocking complete with a satsuma at the bottom on Christmas morning! It was the right decision to get away from it all and do something completely different. I realized that when me and Brad were walking along the beach later that morning.

It was a hot, fairly quiet day, nothing like Christmas Day at all, but I made sure I watched the Oxo advert and made a few comments on Twitter. I've never seen so many tweets come straight back in.

After days spent sunbathing and a couple of trips to a water park and a desert safari, it was New Year's Eve – one I won't forget in a hurry. We went to a party with a guy we'd become friendly with who was a pilot for Emirates at the Arabian Ranches, where I'd been with Lynda all those years beforehand. Even sticking to my sparkling water and lime, it was a good night complete with fireworks at midnight. Lynda would have loved it.

The best thing about not drinking, of course, was the next morning. While everybody else was nursing hangovers, I was greeting 2015 with a clear head. That was a turn up for the books. And exactly two months to the day since Lynda was buried I was back at the grave in Crewkerne telling her everything I'd been up to.

I kicked off the year buying a new soft-top Corvette as

Michael Pattemore

my fun car and a new MacBook computer. Better be careful or I'll be catching Lynda's retail therapy habit – booze was cheaper!

I managed to stay off it (even though I'd stopped the tablets some time back) until just before Lynda's memorial service on 11 February. With hindsight, December and miserable January really were not the best months to be teetotal. One of the worst moments in January was when the new leather dining chairs Lynda had wanted finally got delivered. Far too late for you to enjoy, B. Always the little things once again getting to me. The next time I decide to jump seriously on the wagon – and there will definitely be a next time – I will pick my time better.

Well, Lynda, just as you wanted, all your family and friends had their 'knees up' in London to remember you. Though to be fair, your original idea of organizing it to save them the trip to Crewkerne was a waste of time because most of the 300 people there also turned up to both events anyway!

Once again we all either sang your praises or listened to them being sung at St Stephen Walbrook – old friends, family, colleagues and many famous faces once again.

I bought a new bright blue Italian suit for the occasion and somebody – I can't remember who – made a quip about it being so loud that it could belong to Biggins. He was dressed more soberly than at your funeral, though,

242

and spoke about how proud you'd be of Michael and Robbie.

Speaking at the end of the service, I thanked everybody for being there and recalled how I had stood there at the altar six years and nine months beforehand with Bradley, hardly able to contain my excitement as I was about to marry the most beautiful woman in the world.

'When I saw Lynda walking towards me, I thought my heart would burst with happiness and it did. Now we are here again and now my heart is bursting with sadness,' I said. 'However long we were together would never have been enough.'

I ended by saying, 'You will never be forgotten until the day I die. I love you, Lynda.'

I meant every word all over again.

Earlier, Lesley Joseph read from *There's Something I've Been Dying to Tell You* and Gyles Brandreth spoke about the 'heart and humour' you put into your performances, B, and how believable they always were. He said you'd always be remembered as a 'thoughtful, maternal, generous and fabulous woman' who could also dance and was 'so strong for others'.

The list of all your amazing qualities was endless. Sue Latimer spoke about how you loved life and would always stand strong for the 'underdog, the unfortunate and against the unfair'.

'Your laughter, your smile, your selfless generosity will continue to enrich the lives of everyone lucky enough to have known you,' she added.

Your old flatmate, Felicity McKinney, said that your 'talents were appreciated by all in the industry' and what a 'wonderful and caring godmother' you were to her son Clint. Nickolas Grace told us you were his 'bestest, oldest friend' and the 'consummate actress'.

Your school friend, Jenny Puddiefoot, told how you never forgot your Aylesbury roots and were always willing to give your time and support to benefit others. 'You made my special needs students feel very special,' she added.

Your literary agent, Gordon Wise, read passages from your books. 'While we all know Lynda did more than just fine as an actress,' he said, 'what you might not know is just how successful she was as a writer.'

He went on to explain that you had sold 750,000 books in all and praised your 'wonderful imagination'. He also made everybody laugh by recalling how, on the last time he tried to see you, he took you a souvenir box of fudge and a tea towel from Frinton-on-Sea, where he has a holiday home and where you started your acting career at the local theatre.

You were too ill to see him, but he left the gifts and you

phoned later in the day to thank him. You also told him you'd given me the tea towel because you certainly weren't going to be doing any more washing up where you were going! Still joking so close to the end, B. The fudge and the tea towel are still in the kitchen at home, untouched.

Peter Delaney conducted the service as brilliantly as he had our wedding and your funeral. Everybody laughed again when he said, 'Lynda was not a control freak, but she liked to know what was going on.' Spot on there.

Sadly no white butterflies appeared that day, though, B. Perhaps you were busy up there? You were looking down on us, nevertheless, as I'd had my favourite photo of you blown up and hung high in the church. It is now on the wall in our lounge.

Afterwards we all had drinks and a bite to eat in the church. Then I took all the family out to Nobu for sushi to celebrate Brad's twenty-sixth birthday. You'd have loved it all!

Days later, I was at yet another star-studded do at the Mandarin Oriental Hotel (you were so thrilled that Robbie took you there for a Mother's Day lunch one year, weren't you?) when I collected the Churchill Award on your behalf that had been made posthumously for your charity work. Yet more glory, B.

Still trying to keep busy the rest of the time, I took trips to Dublin for the hair transplant, and to Edinburgh. I had a right good old cry in the cathedral there. I went back to St Bartholomew's on Easter Sunday and then to the grave, where I cried and cried and cried.

Later in April, hoping to find a bit of spiritual enlightenment that didn't come in a bottle, I travelled to the ancient Inca city of Machu Picchu in Peru. My American friends Richard and Shannon organized the trip and invited me along to join their party.

Now you won't be surprised to hear that I wasn't camping or doing any of the serious trekking. Thank God for hotels and minibuses. Nevertheless I did manage to come down with altitude sickness on the first day in Cusco and had to be given oxygen. I wasn't physically sick; I just felt terrible and climbed straight into my bed in the hotel in the Sacred Valley. It was all my own fault because I hadn't read the tourist information that I'd been given when I booked the trip. You know me when you're not around to look after me.

We didn't climb Machu Picchu, but we did climb the smaller but steep 2,693 metres high Wayna Picchu, where we had a bird's eye view of Machu. It really was a surreal place and very spiritual. Up there in the mountains, looking at the sky, you feel so close to something else, another life. The Good Lord? You? All I can say is that it was a phenomenal experience. It wasn't quite so fantastic, though, walking back down all those steps. Scary!

It was very humbling visiting the temples and monuments. But talk about third world poverty. It's everywhere and it does make you realize how lucky we are to live the life that we do. Even my life the way it is at the moment.

As I write this, I am also planning a sort of Lynda Bellingham Pattemore Pilgrimage Tour for the summer. Don't laugh! I will be visiting the place you came from and the places you wanted to go.

In July, I am flying out to Montreal for five days to visit the church that handled your adoption, the hospital you were born in and the house you spent the first six months of your life in before Ruth and Don collected you. I have emailed Marcele, the lady who helped you find your birth mother, Marjorie, who had given you up as soon as you'd been born, and I am hoping to meet her as well.

I can't explain it because I don't know why, but I need to see where it all started, where you came from. Just as it was important for you to finally discover your American birth father, Carl Seymour Hutton, only weeks before you died, and for you to learn that he came from a line of actors. How wonderful that your niece, Martha, traced him through the ship log. He was a crew member and your mother was a passenger. Same old story ... Me and the boys have also met your long lost second cousin, Niki Pittman, as well. It was important for you to tie up all the loose ends at the end of your life, but what a shame it was that you never got to meet her as planned. At least the DNA test you both had put your mind at rest about who you came from.

After Canada, I am heading off on my sixtieth birthday trip in August. Alone. But I am purposely not setting off until the day after 3 August, when I have promised to attend a ceremony with the boys at the Waterside Theatre in Aylesbury where you were brought up. Part of the theatre is being renamed in your memory in the hope that future actors and theatre groups will be inspired by your legacy.

Then I fly to Moscow and St Petersburg, where you filmed *The Romanovs*. I am hoping to meet up with Gleb, the director, there and maybe his son, Ivan. I shall also visit Lyndsay, my sister in Australia, as you wanted me to do. But I am also going to some of the other places we talked about visiting together in The Plan.

Remember how it was you doing *My Tasty Travels* and *Country House Sunday*, when we both discovered beautiful parts of Britain we never knew existed, that set us thinking about places further afield we wanted to visit.

Even before you had cancer, you refused to call it a

bucket list. Your reasoning was that the minute you draw up a list like that it's easy to get preoccupied with just ticking things off it. Not enjoying them properly. That was never our style, was it, Babes?

Far better, you said, to relax and really enjoy doing or seeing the things you're hankering for. You especially fancied going to New Zealand, to see where Jimmy Nesbitt and your friends filmed *The Hobbit*, so that's one of my stops. I will visit India, and especially the Taj Mahal, where you went on your last holiday with your parents and sisters, Japan, Hong Kong, Bangkok, Vancouver and Havana. I'll be travelling for six weeks and it'll be a hectic schedule. Emotional as well without you.

'Hopefully one day . . .' you used to say when we talked about going to these places.

One day never came for you, though, did it, B? And if there is one lesson to be learnt from that it is don't wait for it. Tomorrow may never come; today is the only important one.

CHAPTER 12

THE FIRST ANNIVERSARIES

......

The sun hasn't risen yet and I am standing at Lynda's grave in Townsend Cemetery early on the morning of Sunday, 31 May 2015. Her sixty-seventh birthday. Our seventh wedding anniversary.

The sky is dark, as you'd expect, but not eerie. And as far as I can tell, at 4 a.m., it looks like it's going to be another beautiful day, like yesterday. Not for me though. Or the boys.

The tears are already falling as I look and admire the beautiful white roses lying on her grave. There are lots more than normal, as I specially requested, and the florist delivered them yesterday so they'd be nice and fresh for the double occasion. Occasion! For six phenomenal years it was a double celebration. Nothing left to celebrate now, though, so it's been relegated to an occasion.

I've just realized that I am using a football expression – relegated – when I don't have the slightest interest in football and never have had, being a rugby fan. Perhaps it is because I have been thinking about the Manchester United and England captain, Rio Ferdinand, this month after learning how he lost his wife, Rebecca, to breast cancer. She was only thirty-four. Poor, poor lady; poor, poor man, left with three young children – aged only four, six and nine. A widower. Like me, but nothing like me.

That's another strange thing about bereavement, it connects you somehow to people you don't know at all and are never likely to know. It was the same when the actress Anne Kirkbride died of breast cancer earlier this year at sixty. It just gets you.

In both cases the families kept it quiet until the very end and I completely understand that. I've never met Anne and I don't think Lynda ever did, but of course everybody knows who she is because she played the part of Deirdre in *Coronation Street* for so long. In real life, she sounded a bit like Lynda in the way she always seemed to make time for people less fortunate than herself. Apparently she used to take warm clothes and sandwiches, very quietly, to homeless people in Manchester who were sleeping rough in doorways. My heart goes out to her husband, David Beckett, who was also an actor, as it does to Rio Ferdinand. And their families.

I know just how they are feeling. Well, I say that, but thinking about it, that's not strictly true. Everybody's bereavement is different. All tough, but not the quite the same. How can they be?

What about the poor guy in the street? The low-paid factory worker who loses his wife and suddenly has a young family, not only to work and provide for, but to care for full time as well ?

What happens to his grief when he has no real time to grieve properly? Or the other way round? The poor young mum who loses her husband and breadwinner? What happens to her and the children?

Your own grief binds you to other grief-stricken people. It is a bit like after you've had children, when the news reports on TV become so much harder to watch if they are about children who are starving or have been abused in some way. In part, my own bereavement has helped me to understand why people reacted so strongly when Princess Diana died. Perhaps many of the strangers who lay flowers in these sorts of mass tributes have lost loved ones themselves and that is why they feel the connection.

One thing I am sure of, though, is that all of us in this position will have valued at some time the support we've received from all quarters. From family, our friends and the public. It does help.

Just as it helps, for me, to talk about or even tweet about Lynda. I've taken some stick online for keeping Lynda's twitter page open but, to be honest, it keeps me close to the people who followed her. And that keeps me closer to her, if that makes any kind of sense. It has nothing to do with being mawkish, it just connects me to other people who loved her and talked about her in such an ordinary, straightforward way. Often they've lost loved ones themselves or are perhaps trying to raise money for charity. I really value that connection and they seem to want the connection too, because whenever I stop, people want to know why, and where I am. What's the problem?

Apparently time helps too, though it is far too soon for me to comment on that.

I've been dreading today, 31 May, for weeks. Sundays are hard enough without Lynda's first birthday and our first wedding anniversary falling on my worst day of the week. A double blow. Why couldn't it have been a Friday or a Saturday? I say this, but in my heart I know damn well that it would not make a blind bit of difference. She's gone and, whatever day of the week it is, she's really not coming back to open my cards and presents or to let me surprise her with a romantic weekend away ever again.

Remember our first wedding anniversary, B? When I

picked you up from the *Loose Women* studios and whisked you off to Paris as a surprise? I'd even packed your bag for you. You couldn't believe it! Remember how every time we flew off on holiday, we always had champagne, caviar, oysters (just one for you, a dozen for me) and smoked salmon at the seafood bar at Gatwick or Heathrow first. Then, when we were called to the gate, you'd grab my arm and cuddle up, hanging on to me even as we boarded the plane. I cannot tell you how good that made me feel, having you on my arm like that; both of us laughing, smiling, relaxing even already. And the holiday hadn't even begun. You were so affectionate, but I gave you it back as well, didn't I?

I wasn't laughing quite so much in Paris that year, though, when we were sitting in that outrageously expensive restaurant. There were two menus: one without prices for the lady and a different one with the prices listed for the man who, it had been assumed, would naturally pay the bill! 'Order whatever you like, my lover!' I told you, without batting an eyelid. And you did. Was it foie gras? Probably. I can't remember how big the bill was or how big the tip that I left. I can't honestly even remember what the food tasted like. But I do know that it cost a bloody fortune. And I also know that it was worth every last euro. Oh, to do it all over again ...

Or even to relive our last anniversary – and your last

birthday – spent in Lake Como. Granted, it wasn't one of the very best with your cancer hanging over us. But we at least had hope then. You'd had your operation and we thought you had at least two years to live so we were absolutely bloody determined to make the most of every minute. Which we did.

I can remember Lynda telling her *Yours* magazine readers about the trip to Italy and saying that she couldn't believe it was almost a whole year since she'd been diagnosed with bowel cancer, straight after our previous trip there.

'I know it's a bit of a cliché but I really do appreciate everything I've got so much more now. And I'm so very glad to still be here surrounded by people I love,' she added. Moving words that have become even more moving to me now.

I drove down from London to Crewkerne on Friday in the Range Rover. It was the end of half-term week, I think, and the journey was horrendous. The motorway was chock-a-block but the traffic coming in the opposite direction, towards London, was even worse. It was well into the evening before I arrived at my mum's old house, where I stayed overnight. I came up to the grave at lunchtime on the Saturday. There was nobody in there at all so it was lovely and peaceful. I checked on the flowers and the handwritten cards that the florist had put with them, as I'd asked her to do.

One of the cards carried the words that will eventually be inscribed on the pale headstone when all the planning regulations have been fulfilled and it is ready to be erected:

LYNDA BELLINGHAM PATTEMORE
The curtain went up 31st May 1948
The final curtain came down 19th October 2014
Actress, author and presenter
A unique loving mother and wife
Ten years wasn't enough

And underneath I had written:

Happy birthday and happy wedding anniversary from
your loving husband Michael XXX

The other card contained a simple verse:

God saw that you were getting tired;
   a cure was not to be
So he put his arms around you and whispered
   'come with me'

With tearful eyes I watched you suffer and saw
    you fade away,
Although I loved you dearly, I could not make
    you stay
A golden heart stopped beating
Hard working hands to rest
God broke our hearts to prove to us
He only takes the best.

                        Love Michael XXX

And it is true. You were the best, B. Nothing more certain.

I am not a bitter person but losing someone like I lost Lynda does test you. You look at life sometimes and hear about people who don't give a fig about anybody else and they live to be a ripe old age. Life ain't always fair. It's just one of those things. You just have to try and console yourself, believing words and ideas like the ones expressed in this verse. Only the good die young and all that. Although, of course, some would say that Lynda wasn't that young. And compared to Rio's Rebecca she wasn't. Sometimes, as well, it is best just not to think too much at all . . .

For a good while, I just sat on a bench in the early Saturday afternoon sunshine, looking round the graveyard and crying my eyes out. Time really doesn't stand still and when I looked at my watch, I couldn't believe that an hour had gone by.

I am praying to God that before the actual one-year anniversary date – Monday, 19 October 2015 – the headstone will be up and the grave will be complete. The cemetery superintendent, Nigel Peters, does a superb job down there but I've often felt that it looks as if we haven't bothered about Lynda's grave without a proper headstone in place.

I always wanted you to be the star of the graveyard, B, like you were in life. I am sorry if that sounds harsh or unfair on the graves of all the other wives, husbands, mums, dads, grandmas, granddads, aunties and uncles lying there, my own dad included. Or unfeeling towards all their loved ones. But that is just how I feel and I am being honest. So many people knew and loved Lynda and if anybody comes to look at her grave, I want them to be able to see straight away which one it is.

I have also sponsored a couple of trees. Crewkerne Council is cutting down the old ones and replanting young ones to grow in their place. New life, a bit like mine. I've bought a bench as well which will carry a plaque in memory of Lynda. I know she would have been quite happy with a basic, ecologically friendly coffin and burial, but I would not do it. End of. She knew that. I wanted her to be somewhere beautiful and she is. The countryside surrounding the cemetery is stunning.

Later on Saturday I drive over to see my old business partner, Roger, at Haselbury Mill to finalize the arrangements for our trip to Normandy. We are going to visit the war graves for the anniversary of the D-Day landings.

Roger goes every year after he started taking his dad, an old Second World War veteran, in the early 1990s. He first asked me months ago and I have finally decided to take him up on the offer. Perhaps it isn't the cheeriest place in the world to be heading but, in a way, it matches my mood.

Early Sunday morning, a taxi picks up me and my stepbrother Michael, and I ask Sarah the driver to stop at the cemetery gates so I can have a little bit more time with Lynda. I get out and come to the graveside. Just for five minutes. My real anniversary visit was yesterday when I had more time to sit alone and reflect.

A few minutes later, Michael follows me to the graveside. It makes it easier having him with me here today, I feel less alone. I tell Lynda that I love her and I miss her, shed a few more tears and then say goodbye. Me and Michael walk out of the dim, deserted cemetery together, get back in the taxi and head for the Mill, where our party of thirteen is setting off nice and early to catch the 8 a.m. ferry from Poole to Cherbourg. Some of us are being driven by Roger in the old Daimler he uses for wedding receptions held at the hotel. Others are in a big American lorry, which is pulling a trailer containing another old American troop carrier. None of it turns out to be trouble free, though. First we have problems with a wheel flying off; then a drama with a gearbox. Best laid plans and all that . . .

We've hired a chateau in Normandy, where we settle in and make our plans. Tomorrow we will visit the Airborne Museum in the square of Sainte Mère-Église, a few miles from the D-Day landing beaches and facing the church where the American paratrooper, John Steele, famously landed and got stuck on the tower. Sainte Mère-Élise was the first village to be liberated on D-Day and Steele was made famous in the film *The Longest Day*.

I will light a candle for Lynda in the church. She'd like that. Both the war connection with her dad and the connection to the film too. It seems fitting somehow. Besides, I find being in churches a real comfort since she died. The calm, the peace, the connection with another life.

Tonight, though, we need to eat. Like everyone else, I am ravenous and so we head out for an evening meal at a pizzeria. Afterwards I stand up and make an announcement to the table: 'Can we have a toast to Lynda, please?' I don't need to ask again. Everybody raises their glasses. 'To Lynda,' I manage to say with the biggest lump in my throat. And after we all take a drink, I go outside on my own to have another cry.

I texted the boys earlier in the day to say 'Hello stepsons; it's your stepdaddy here.' Michael rang me back, but Robbie texted back as he was working. I don't really know if they're OK or not. I don't know how we should all be feeling at this stage. What is normal?

I might have lost a wonderful wife, but I try never to forget that they have lost a wonderful mother too. It is hard for us all and it is still early days. All I can say right now is that I definitely did the right thing coming away to France to spend such an emotional day. It would have been so easy to sit at home and wallow. Sometimes it feels like I could do that for the rest of my life. Then other days are nothing like that.

Since this first anniversary has passed, life has gone on, of course. And much of it has been just as emotional. There's been my trip to Montreal to trace Lynda's roots, and my birthday travels. Neither was exactly how I could have imagined it would be. But isn't that life all over? Full of surprises, good and bad. Or sometimes just ordinary. Mundane. Run of the mill.

And now there's the future. My future. Alone for now but maybe not for long. Who knows? Maybe Yvonne, the medium, has the right answer; maybe not. Only time will tell. While I am on this earth, though – and that is not something I take for granted any more as I once used to – I intend to follow on in one set of Lynda's footsteps at least. I am talking about her charity work not her acting!

You taught me well, B, so I have carried on some of what you left off. I have officially been made a patron of Action Against Cancer and a patron of Bowel Cancer UK, as well as helping out Barnardo's in their appeal for foster carers. I've even officially set off the hundreds of female runners in bright pink T-shirts at a Race for Life event in July, in Taunton. It was organized by Cancer UK to raise money for breast cancer research. I would have done the run myself but men are banned from taking part. Honestly!

So much has been going on that I almost forgot to add that your iconic Oxo advert 'And Michael . . . Remember Preston?' won a BAFTA this year. You never know, you might get that posthumous Oscar yet, B! The Royal Horticultural Society has had a special hybrid tea rose grown and named after you as well. It was unveiled at Hampton Court Palace Flower Show in June. Although not white, I think you'd like its golden apricot colour, large petals and light spicy perfume.

In your memory, I am also partly sponsoring a season's scholarship for a young actor at Frinton Summer Theatre, where you gave your first professional performance in

1969. The first of many. A blue plaque has been erected there to mark your achievement.

Who knows what I will do next? Until we meet again, my lover, it's all keeping me busy and out of too much mischief. Just as you wanted. Rest in peace, Babes.

AFTERWORD

P.S. MY LOVER

......

If I ever need any reminder of how hard this past year has been without you, B, I only have to read through this book again.

Like you, I've never had a problem laying my emotions on the line, but it is strange to see them written down in black and white for posterity. The phenomenal highs of loving you and the devastating lows of losing you. As we both know, life changes all the time and, bit by bit, we change with it. It's the same with grief. I can see that looking back through these pages and comparing how I felt a year ago to how I feel now. I wouldn't want to go back to those excruciatingly raw first days without you for anything. So it must be true that time heals, even if it's only a little bit. Rest assured, I'm not over you yet, Babes! Far from it.

But, as you so wisely put it, throughout your illness, you can never see clearly when you're in the eye of the storm and you need to wait for the dust to settle. Well, my lover, as ever, you were absolutely right. The dust has settled a fair bit now and although the pain of losing you hasn't disappeared, I no longer expect it to.

Not a day has yet gone by when I haven't cried and wished you were back here with me (though not with the pain). Even if it's only been so that you could fill out the planning application forms for my properties again in your beautiful handwriting! You know what my left-handed scrawl is like, but it's had to do ... Or to fill up the fridge and cook up steak and chips for a midweek dinner. Only healthy chips, of course, done in the low fat fryer! These days, I buy bags of steaks and chicken breasts from the supermarket and they can still be there, untouched, a week later. By the way, the boys *still* don't close the freezer door properly so I've slammed a warning notice on it. I'm not as soft with them as you, B.

The snack cupboard is completely empty as well, after I chucked out a half-empty box of M&S mini-mince pies when I realized the use-by date was December 2014. Bought in hope ... Remember when that cupboard was groaning with goodies in case anybody fancied a snack watching television? I don't think I've touched a salt and vinegar crisp in a year. Or a bar of Cadbury's Dairy Milk, our favourite. Even the wine rack has run low and these days you'd be sharing a bottle of sparkling water with me if you were still around. Yes, that's absolutely right, B, I did say sparkling water!

Once again, I am back on the wagon after realizing how much wine I've been getting through in your absence. Without you, it's bloody lonely here and, as early as mid-afternoon some days, I found myself coming downstairs from the office and into the kitchen to pour my first proper drink of the day. Bad habit. I can't pretend it didn't helped blur my grief and help me relax but, ultimately, the wine bottle is no real friend in need, as you discovered yourself when Jean had her accident. You can't depend on it without suffering the consequences, so I've knocked it on the head for now at least. We'll see how long it lasts this time ... Perhaps I really should have learnt to enjoy a nice British cup of tea like you did. Remember how you missed the kettle when we had the kitchen refurbished and had a hot water tap installed? A pleasant little ritual gone, you grumbled at first.

Well, I've had to get used to lots of little rituals disappearing this past year. The reminders of them are still everywhere, like the pile of books lying on your bedside cabinet all waiting to be read before we turned the light out at night – John Grisham, Ian Rankin, James Patterson ... One even has the jacket flap holding your place on pages ten and eleven. Didn't get very far into that one, did you, Babes? Every week, the cleaners dust round them and my Corvette handbook lying next to them. I can't bring myself to move them just yet. Daft, I know, but it's just the way it is.

I can't pretend it hasn't been painful writing this book (on the computer, not by hand, you won't be surprised to hear) at times but, if nothing else, it has forced me to face up to things. No sticking my head in the sand and thinking you're going to walk through that door because you ain't.

But I've survived to tell the tale, even if it's been by the skin of my teeth sometimes. Bereavement really is a journey. Just like our life together. Up and down, thankfully more up than down for most of our ten wonderful years together.

I have to say that this year has been much more down than up for me, though. So much has changed, even things you wouldn't expect. Believe it or not, I've been putting off all the little DIY jobs – I am only just getting round to them now. I used to be such a stickler as well, didn't I? Remember how I hated seeing lights not working? Well, if I tell you that the low voltage recess bulb in the kitchen above the oven went soon after you died and I only replaced it at the end of June, it'll give you some idea of how lax I've become. It was only a five-minute job as well, but I kept putting it off until tomorrow. Well, as we discovered, you just have to live for today. Seize it, just like the Yanks say.

That's what I tried to explain to a couple of neighbours, who neither of us had ever met when you were alive. I probably never would have either, if you hadn't written *There's Something I've Been Dying to Tell You.*

I was just heading off on my early morning walk round the manor when a guy, about my age I guess, saw me from his apartment window and came out to speak to me.

After introducing himself, he explained that he'd read your book, B, and wondered if I would speak to his wife who, like you, had been diagnosed with stage four colon cancer and was about to start chemotherapy treatment.

'Give me your address, let me go for my walk and I will come round on my way back,' I promised, and I did. Sitting down with them, I spent an hour and a half, maybe even two hours, going over and over all the positives I could think of in the hope of reassuring them that it didn't all have to end the way it did for you, B. Us even.

I've spent my whole life turning negatives to positives. I always believed there was a solution to everything – except, in your case, there wasn't, was there? That's still hard for me to accept.

Nevertheless, I told the couple the truth when I told them not to think the worst. 'It is not going to happen overnight,' I assured them. 'And the great thing about medical science is that it constantly advances,' I went on. 'Everybody is different and everything depends on the type of tumour you've got and how long you've had it. If you're lucky, you may even be suitable for trial drugs. One thing is for sure, you ain't going to die today and you ain't going to die tomorrow. You could go on another five, six or even ten years,' I continued quite honestly. Just as we hoped and prayed you would, didn't we, B?

I meant everything I said and I really hope I gave them a reason to be optimistic. After all, that is all you can do, all you have in their position. We've walked in their shoes and we know. Well now, I'm walking alone and, thankfully, I am still upright. You used to say your illness made you a better person. It's a bit of a long shot, but perhaps ultimately bereavement has even done the same to me. I hope I've always had time for other people, but I probably have more now. Bloody hell, I'll be retraining and becoming a social worker next, Babes! Well, perhaps not . . .

To take a leaf out of your book, though, Babes, I am trying to use this latest life experience, this bereavement, to help others as you always did.

I've been asked recently what advice I would give to people in my position and I think I'd have to say:

Number One: Keep busy, even if some days that only means putting one foot in front of the other. Even on your worst days, give yourself a goal, cook a meal, load the dishwasher. You've got to keep going. No good wallowing in bed because you'll only feel worse.

Number Two: Don't be afraid to cry alone or in public. There's no shame in it. True friends and family understand and only want to help you work through your grief. Far worse to bottle it up because it will only come out in a torrent at the end.

Number Three: Take it at your own pace. If you don't want to get rid of clothes, jewellery, half-full bags of sweets or packets of fags that make you feel close to somebody you've lost, then don't. Wait until you feel good and ready. Equally, if you want a clear-out straight after the funeral, then do it.

Number Four: Talk, talk, talk about your loved one until you're blue in the face. Remember the good times as well as the bad and you'll find yourself laughing or at least smiling as well as crying. It balances your emotions.

Number Five: Don't be ashamed to go for counselling. I personally haven't felt I've needed it, but I know people who have and it has helped them.

Writing this book has been therapeutic for me. Perhaps keeping a diary and writing down your feelings might help. You will be surprised, looking back, how you have moved on, even if you don't think so.

Number Six: Plan ahead. Time can weigh very heavily when you're suddenly alone, so it is important to fill your time and have events to look forward to. I hate being in the apartment at weekends so I have planned to be away as much as I can, visiting different friends and family. Otherwise the days seem endless.

Number Seven: This is really Lynda's tip, but it works for me. Turn a negative into a positive by doing something to help others going through what you've already experienced. Volunteer for a charity close to your heart or take part in a fundraising event for them.

Number Eight: Last but not least, remember there are no set rules when coping with bereavement. It is different for every one of us. So if none of my advice here is right for you, just ignore it. Do it your own way. I wish you well on your journey.